Pyramids and Grapefruit
A Travel Journal

Pyramids
and Grapefruit

A Travel Journal

Sylvie Nisbet

The Book Guild Ltd.
Sussex, England

The Book Guild Ltd.
25 High Street,
Lewes, Sussex

First published 1994
© Sylvie Nisbet 1994
Set in Palatino
Typesetting by Southern Reproductions (Sussex)
East Grinstead, Sussex
Printed in Great Britain by
Antony Rowe Ltd.
Chippenham, Wiltshire.

A catalogue record for this book is
available from the British Library

ISBN 0 86332 906 3

CONTENTS

For my parents,
Christine and Ulric

INTRODUCTION

All my life I have been a potter, but during the 50s and 60s I took a three month holiday every winter, as there was always a lull in my business during the months of January, February and March after the busy Christmas period. Initially looking for sunshine as an escape from the British winter, I travelled to the Middle East, a region far more accessible at that time than it is today, and quickly became enamoured with the whole area.

I hope I have written a book about the Middle East which will raise a wan smile of familiarity from anyone who knows the region, or better still be informative and useful to those yet to travel there. Then, as now, the conflict of religions dominated many of the countries; with no particular religion of my own other than the belief that there is only one God, I travelled with an open mind and a neutral, hopefully receptive attitude to the religions of others, be they Moslem, Christian or Jew.

I attempted to understand the hatred which so often divides cultures on the basis of religion, and always rejoiced when I came across basic kindness and friendship overcoming such divisions.

Like all travel books, mine provided an escape and a learning experience, both in the doing and the writing, and my travels themselves came to a natural end when I found I had reached the state of happiness for which I had travelled so frequently and so far to find.

Egypt

Going abroad alone seemed an exciting prospect when I planned this holiday. At twenty, an only child, instilled with lofty morals by my parents, I longed to escape or rather learn about life for myself. It was just before Christmas 1955 and the piles of parcels in Victoria Station reminded me of the festivities I would be missing. My family, an American mother, an English father, were in New York for the time being. We had already exchanged seasonal greetings by telephone and letter. Now I was free to go away for as long as my money (five shillings a day, I hoped) would last. To travel was my decision, I thought it was the right one.

A train came in with an expressionless grey-faced driver at the controls. As he passed me, seeing my look of concentration, he smiled. I said to myself, that's all I've got, my only protection on this trip: the knowledge that people are touchable, that's all I've learnt of life so far.

Our train to Paris started and crossed the bridge over the Thames. Barges were busy, smoke billowed from the power station. We could see for a moment into Battersea Dogs' Home where the creatures pranced around their yards. Sitting next to me a schoolboy on his way to visit his father in Paris asked how long the trip would take, how many miles we would travel, if the sea was rough, all questions to disguise *his* worry of travelling alone.

At Newhaven a steward stepping out on deck to check our departure shook hands with one of the crew, in the other hand he carried the bell. After a few words he shivered and went inside vigorously ringing the signal for lunch. The ship's gentle rocking turned to lurching as it reached the open sea. An Arab who had been eating bananas suddenly got up from the table leaving the skins in a tangled heap. The waiter watched, sharpening a knife on the bottom of a plate, then as more passengers left the dining room, he started screwing the port holes closed. The sounds, the smells, the slight bump of the ship docking, so far the routine had been familiar to me from other journeys.

Dieppe porters in navy blue scampered towards an official who blew a whistle and shouted, '*Alors! Alors!*' The porters' faces were wizened, ears flattened against their cropped heads, foreheads wrinkled, they swung lanterns as they ran.

Passengers on the stationary train called out, 'Here we are! Here we are!' An American led a procession of loaded porters. An Italian carrying a biscuit tin tied with string asked directions. He was in the wrong compartment, then I found, on the wrong train. The platform was at last clear. The guard waved a flag. Nothing happened.

'What are we waiting for?' called a passenger.

'*Un coup d'air!*' replied the guard.

Through holes in the engine's smoke dripping over the windows I caught a glimpse of geese, black hens and some apples left on the trees, it was a strip of French countryside I had already seen two years ago, on my way to study in Paris. Where was the feeling I wanted so much, that my holiday had begun?

In the Paris youth hostel's hot little communal room I sat by the Christmas tree. Its moulting needles made the floor gritty under people's boots. A Glasgow furniture dealer asked a German girl if the stockings he had bought for his sister were a nice shade.

'Yah! Ha! Ha!'

A Spanish guitar player and his song almost drowned conversation. Heavily dressed, small, French couples came in from their tents to cook supper. A German boy sat on a stool under the light, his body a loop of arms, a loop of legs, dressed in black, he was like a plant in a forest.

'We in Germany,' he said, 'were bombed three times. I was dug out after three hours, six hours, and the last, after thirty hours. The terrible thing was coming out and finding everything going on as usual. After an experience like that you expect the world to have changed. Worst of all was the disillusionment of my father. He was such a big shot to us during the war, you know, he would come home on leave once a year, he would be covered in medals. We did not have much to eat and he used to bring us things we hadn't even dreamed about. I respected him like a god. When the war ended I saw him come home a bum, looking dirty. We saw him doing deals for cigarettes, then he started drinking. I found I didn't know him anymore . . . .' To delay his return to Germany the boy sold his watch and waving the thousand franc note declared, 'A week of life, ten days perhaps.' I sympathised. 'You're soft. You're an *idealist*,' he scoffed.

The Louvre, the Rodin Museum, Les Tuilleries, I visited the places I loved before taking the train to Nice. There the hostel was in the old part. The *mére d'auberge* had made the flowered curtains and quilts for the wooden bunks. Her black poodle took no notice of visitors, he walked around us disdainfully as though his legs wouldn't bend. Two Dutch students at the hostel found speaking English and French difficult. Three times a day they fried two eggs each then sat wondering what to do next. A group of young Parisian boys came in late and got up the latest. They crept about on thick crêpe-soled shoes while playing a harmonica. They could not decide who was going to cook the soup. The Dutch boys looking on, finally made themselves understood. 'We have never seen Frenchmen drinking *milk*.'

The French boys boasted that they drank a bottle of wine each *en route*, 'Even more,' one added. Bernard seemed to be the French boys' leader.

'Chewing gum,' he called the cheese. After their meal they climbed on the bench to study a map on the wall. Bernard traced his trip to Stockholm.

'Is it interesting?' his friends asked.

Bernard replied, 'It is interesting enough for a Parisian to see once.'

In the afternoon I sat on a beach where a distinct puff-puff line of clouds across the horizon looked as though a train had passed. The day before the sun had been hot and people swam. Today only a fur-coated girl and her monkey wearing a sweater walked along the Promenade des Anglais.

Next came Italy. From the Florence hostel a train went straight to the Uffizi Galleries. When I got there a museum guard kept interrupting and advising me to hurry on this, the once-a-week free day: there were forty more rooms of paintings I should see.

On my return to the hostel I talked to an American girl called Anna who had also been to the Uffizi. Hearing how thwarted I felt, she offered to lend me her students' pass so I could go free, as often as I wished. We had supper and Anna told me about herself. 'I work in a restaurant all day. Yeh, waitress. By the time I get home at night I'm dead tired but gee whiz, I want to paint!'

In the yellowish warm light the towers and turrets of Florence could have looked the same at any season. Bells rang the hour with times so varied that one took over from another, often many heavy old bells were ringing slowly out of turn. All day I kept walking as if I were afraid I might miss something. The rare moments I relaxed and listened to the bells or noticed the reflections in the river, I knew, at the back of my mind, that I would miss nothing, that in time everything would come to me.

We crossed the Ponte Vecchio and picnicked in gardens frequented by lonely old men who hid behind the many statues and whistled hopefully at every woman. At *Poste Restante* we found nuns could push harder than anyone to reach the counter. Only shopkeepers we made friends with for a few days. The richness of Florence offered Anna and I enough to share. In the Academia, in front of Michelangelo's David, Anna assured me. 'His hands are too big but you get used to them.' And at night I would fall asleep instantly on the hostel's hard straw palliasse.

'Big Ben has stopped! Worst winter England's had in years!' A hearty Australian in the Naples hostel gave me the first news from home. Though a cloud covered Vesuvius the weather was mild this far south. Soon Anna arrived at the hostel and we talked as if continuing the conversation from our last meeting in Florence. She was less bothered by rain and cold than by people; anyone south of Rome she called, 'Insensitive and animal.' Children who begged or threw stones and men who stared and followed us horrified her.

Anna was an artist and the beings she sketched in her notebooks were abstract. 'I never use pure colour,' Anna elucidated, 'they are painted later in oils on oriental paper.' I thought she could have created them just as well in New York, her home town. She loved her paintings and carried many with her. Someone should have painted Anna. Epstein might have modelled her. She had big brown eyes, olive skin and long black hair, which enabled her to pass for a native in any country touching the Mediterranean. The scenes in the narrow streets: children listening to a wandering singer, a man selling second-hand shoes strung on a pole, roosters scratching between the cobbles, a donkey tied to a door, that's what I would have painted in Naples if I could draw, not Anna's disconnected fantasies.

'I'm not the same after going to Pompeii,' announced Anna. I agreed. A cast of one of the victim's bodies, arms raised protectively over his head, summarized the tragedy and this dramatic find was the first thing one saw there. 'The richest house' had high-ceilinged bedrooms decorated with painted panels of birds and flowers and pornographic subjects that only men were allowed to examine. The guide explained how varying temperatures had been controlled and maintained in the steam baths where casts of the contorted bodies of two slaves who had not escaped Vesuvius' eruption lay side by side. Cobbles in the narrow streets were deeply worn by cart wheels, stepping stones had provided crossing places in bad weather. A cypress stirred by the wind in a deserted garden made me shudder as though I had seen a ghostly figure. Neither of us had been so affected by the past before visiting Pompeii.

The following day when we saw a poster showing blue sky and pyramids we simultaneously cried, 'Let's go!' The travel agent in whose window the poster was displayed, booked us on a Turkish ship leaving for Alexandria in four days. A berth, fourth class, without food cost six pounds. 'Sure we'll be sea-sick,' Anna encouraged economy. 'What do we want food for?'

Until the ship sailed we stayed in a pension near Naples where bourgainvillea crushed the high garden walls, unkempt palms obscured windows and cats prowled through the underbush. 'Looks like a real rough place from outside,' observed Anna. From our room we could see fishermen laying their nets in the sea. Buses came and went over distant hills while villagers with folded arms waited in the square all day. Leading down to the square were steep steps, over them house shutters almost touched. Bird cages, potted ferns or drying umbrellas hung out of windows. Strings of washing criss-crossed from house to house. We could hear singing voices, screeching ones and the sound of a guitar. A fisherman going from door to door stopped at our pension to sell the cook a live octopus. When he tried to wrap it up, its arms kept coming out of the newspaper. Anna and I watching, laughed until we cried.

The wet beach was littered with rotten oranges, cacti limbs and old shoes filling with sand. The sea made the noise like the heavy breathing of someone asleep. Layer upon layer of cloud buried the sun. My walking alone upset Anna. She thought me moody. 'My first impression of you was that you are unsociable,' she informed me.

I said, 'That will be your last one too. But I'm not.' I needed solitude. Meanwhile we had decided to go to Egypt together, a country I wouldn't have visited on my own.

We were half-way to Egypt. An oddly warm breeze blew over the sea and sunlight spilled from clouds making patches on the water. Occasionally one of the ship's passengers would stop by my chair and talk. A Turk described his country's marvellous ceramics, (ceramics were my business). He insisted all Arabs are thieves. Later he was replaced by an Arab who declared, 'Turks are dangerous.' The Arab considered it fortunate I was going to Cairo instead of Istanbul.

The next passer-by (whose business was air-conditioning), taking deep breaths turned to me, 'It's the wind of the desert now,' he murmured. My holiday had begun!

We were twenty-four hours behind schedule due to a storm. The crew had brought us crumbling delicacies in their pockets which we were too sick to eat. I lost two days from my life; then, the roughest weather over, a steward carried me on deck and laid me in a chair. With fresh air I recovered. Anna remained below, our mute, thick-set steward, Mustapha, sat by her with a bucket ready.

At night it seemed to be the stars which rocked as we floated suspended in blackness. Turkish sailors talked and grinned and leaned on the rail. The famished sound of waves mixed with the rumble-tumble of the engines. All I could see were lines of empty deck chairs, a row of electric lights, the decks washed clean, still wet from the storm, and back and forth two German boys walked arm in arm singing 'Silent Night'.

A Turkish officer interrupted my meditation to discuss Zola and Maugham; the latter he preferred. He explained, '*Big* ideas aren't needed. A writer must appeal to the masses. This is the twentieth century!' I declined his invitation for a drink so he added, 'You think you are seeing life. You sit here alone and stare at the sea. You will never understand people this way.'

'We are in Cairo. The children . . . .' I could write no more of my letter until I returned to the hotel. As soon as they had seen me, the dozens of children playing on the grass rushed over to my park bench, not to beg, simply to look into my green eyes and at my auburn hair. I smiled. They all smiled. That was all. I was overcome and retreated.

We came from Alexandria in a three-hour drive by bus across the desert. Even the sandscape changed, sometimes we saw goats wandering, sometimes we wondered if they were bushes or really droopy-headed animals waiting in the sun. Anna spotted the pyramids and pointed them out. The minute yellow triangles gave me a strange thrill; they represented a world as different from mine as I could imagine. Then as the road wound closer we caught sight again, now enormous and grand, they dominated my thoughts.

The square block of our hotel had rooms as high as they were wide and halls open to the sky. Its stone floor was paved with slabs grave-stone size. Servants watched through key holes used for no other purpose and the fat sweaty manager slept at his desk almost in the dark. Taps dripped, mattresses were beaten and rooms swept with long twig brooms. At night, light came through the shutters in a way Anna called, 'Very Eastern'. Anna insisted there would be no bed-bugs when I wanted to buy DDT. The first night in Cairo, I cried out as I was bitten. 'The strength of psychological suggestion,' she snorted. No sympathy was wasted on my red spots the next day either. Anna never experienced such problems: insects ignored her, she ignored them.

Our hotel was at the corner of Station Square where, with a

bitter clanging warning, trams crawled after each other and battle-scarred Cairo taxis emitted endless toots. I sat in the wide recess of the window warmed by the sun even at an early hour. A cat rolled on its back in the grassy square below. A child hopped over the low railing and made a rush at the sleek creature. In three bounds the cat was out of the boy's reach. The child kicked one leg after the other in the air, his shoes flew in opposite directions. He and the cat lay still, watching the circling cars.

By the hotel door a stall selling oranges, a wooden-runged one for bread and another cooking sweet potatoes provided our breakfast. One-man businesses thrived with a handful of purple sunglasses or a crate of lemons. An Arab boy had a puppy to sell, he carried the skin-and-bone dog slung over his shoulder. At a likely spot, he dropped it on the pavement where it lay for a moment, dazed, and then shook itself making a cloud of dust. He had no need to tie it up, it sat in his shadow. A stall-holder who laughed the most suddenly produced a knife but the fight ended when another man was kicked in the shins. He hobbled tragically to the kerb to sit down and the others, resting against each other, crowded around to look at his leg. I could not remember who was fighting whom.

People hung on the buses, on the carts, on the trams. This excess of humanity should have made progress impossible. All afternoon eagles drifted stiffly in the sky, hovering as if hung on invisible strings. At last it happened, a taxi accidentally got caught on a tram. Innumerable drivers and vehicles might as well have been entangled for the chaos it caused. Finally a policeman separated the offending machines. Life resumed its momentum, the trams clanged, clanged away, the sun sank a bit lower. It was still just as hot.

We had been in Cairo several days when Anna remarked, 'We haven't seen the Nile!'

I said, 'Yes, we have.'

'Well, we haven't gazed into it anyhow.' We did see the Nile and the pyramids and the Egyptian museum, over and over again. Then we went south.

For six hours after leaving Cairo we were tightly wedged between passengers. Some at last got off the train and we had the wooden bench to ourselves. Fine sand was all over me, even in my throat, I found, when I tried to speak. Anna and I were the only Europeans in this third class carriage. Other women held their black covering closely so that only their eyes showed. I understood the practicality of their clothes now. Two Arabs squatted against the door. One rubbed his toe, then his nose absent-mindedly, at every movement the material of his gown fell into new crescent-moon-shaped creases. I noticed their eyes gleamed with the brightness ours have only when filled with tears.

A big black Arab entertaining the compartment with his jokes, drew out a gun and flourished it to illustrate part of his story. My look of alarm made him roar with laughter. Near us a girl of six or seven, standing in the aisle, gave me a timid encouraging smile. She was dressed in an old flour sack, tied at the waist with string. I offered her a piece of bread but she touched her head and her heart in a gesture of polite refusal. I had not yet learned that everyone here was hungry, and that only if the gift were offered three times, to make sure it was offered genuinely, would it be accepted. The Arab with the gun watched. Roaring, smiling, he shouted for the coffee man and ordered a glassful for me. Before the coffee came, reassured, I had fallen asleep.

We arrived in Luxor at 2 a.m. with no plans, no expectations or knowledge of what we would find except the Hotel France. Every town seemed to have a Hotel France that charged two shillings a night and changed the sheets for foreigners. This may not sound like an entry into Paradise but it was. The next morning we breakasted on the hotel balcony. The sunrise was gentle, the air smelled sweet, camels loaded with grass passed silently on the dirt road. Time as we knew it didn't exist. I must have spent weeks and weeks in Luxor that winter doing absolutely nothing for the first and last time in my life. A band started to play in the next square. A boy carrying a cage of rabbits on his head ran towards the music. I could see his rabbits stop nibbling their salad in surprise, forgotten stalks stuck out of their mouths. Six black-gowned women paid no attention, they walked the other way balancing tins of water on their heads. Between the houses, between the palms, beyond the Nile I could just see, lay Thebes. Over there life and greenness ended, there where the Valley of the Kings began.

For a pass to the sites we applied to the Inspector of Ancient Monuments who was himself an archaeologist. Poinsettias that I knew as potted plants at Christmas were, in his garden, giant trees. I asked if he continued to excavate during the summer. Such interesting work made one forget heat and these discomforts he said, though among his treasured scarabs and ancient pottery collection, the Plymouth Rock chickens he had imported from America were his prize possessions.

The temple of Karnak, next to the village of the same name, was half an hour's walk from Luxor. Along the road children cried, 'Good morning Madame. Give *baksheesh*.' And when the words produced no reaction, they ran away laughing. We trudged through the heat, the Egyptian women, I noticed, gave the impression they glided. The men here wore more solid colours than in Cairo, more black or royal blue robes, topped with larger white turbans.

Karnak village, a few mud-brick houses under the palms, framed the gateway and the obelisk of the ancient temple. A drive lined with dozens of ram-headed sphinxes led to the ruins. Built at first as a shrine, the whole had become a complex of temples, each pharaoh adding to or altering his predecessor's work. Aknaton's rule and temple dedicated to a single god was only a brief interlude in the two thousand years of Karnak's history devoted to the worship of a myriad of gods and goddesses. Remains of crude brick ramps on which the stones were heaved into place can still be found. The great hypostyle hall contains 134 columns, 21 metres high, their capitals, it is said, could hold 100 standing men. Here the statues, stiff and staring, however remarkable, could not evoke the ghosts of Pompeii. In Karnak, I felt only an awareness of tremendous age between our times.

Anna acquired a guide, son of a shop-keeper, who said he had nothing else to do and would look after us. He had fallen in love with Eleanor Parker when a film, *The Valley of the Kings*, starring her and Robert Taylor had been made in Luxor. The episode had converted him to Christianity. A cross, recently tattooed on his arm, and Eleanor Parker's autograph, were displayed as references.

We were told to meet him by the ferry at 'nine exactly' for

our trip to the valley. We should have interpreted him as meaning 'after ten'. Finally he arrived and the ferry rowed us across the Nile. On the eastern shore, mobbed by donkey owners, we had to choose quickly. The guide and I found ourselves on big white donkeys that started trotting as soon as we were up. Two men placed Anna on a little brown one that followed ours. She had neglected to tell us that she had never ridden. Cries of 'Help! Help!' mingled with the donkey's mournful he-haws. 'What's he doing?' she screamed.

'We pass his home,' called back the guide authoritatively. I thought it more likely he had noticed a female donkey tethered in a nearby field.

We entered a moon-world of bleakness and hot bright light, and shading our eyes, let the jogging donkeys find their way between the hills of stones from abandoned excavations. Three drivers slept in their machines outside the main tombs while their passengers explored. That day no one else came by donkey.

Walls and ceilings of the tombs had been smoothly finished for frescoes or hieroglyphics with which they were covered. Only on the rough passages descending to them did one notice the marks of workmen's tools. Each tomb complex was hollowed out from the core of the rock, each had its own style and dominant colour. The largest and most magnificent tomb we saw belonged to Seti I which, when discovered in 1817, contained only the Pharaoh's empty alabaster sarcophagus. Scenes from the Book of the Dead cover the tomb's 100 metre length. Some gods carried an eye to protect them against evil. One room's ceiling was superbly painted with astrological figures. Another room's murals had been blackened by the candles of early Christians hiding there. Lucky was the Pharaoh, helped by the sun god to reach the hereafter, surrounded by his earthly possessions: he was able to eat and drink and live and rule eternally.

Exhausted, afterwards we sat by our donkeys and ate oranges in silence. Our guide had long ago given up singing 'Deep in the Heart of Texas' and now suggested shortening the trip to Deir el Barari by crossing the hills. I considered this temple to be over-restored though our guide argued that every Egyptian ruin should be rebuilt for tourists. With this on my mind I ran to mount my donkey, noticed a young English man watching and, distracted, missed. I vaulted right over the animal. Mortified, I clambered on without looking back. In Egypt I had forgotten I was among strangers, this abrupt reminder caused me a moment's homesickness.

By afternoon we were approaching the colossus of Memanon, a pair of statues twenty metres high, seated on either side of the dirt track, alone in the empty plain. Whether it was planned or pure folly only Anna's donkey knew, for just then, with the terrible noise peculiar to him, he burst into a gallop. She flew by me, her expression rigid, her fists clenching his mane, her own hair uncoiled and waving. The guide's donkey leapt as if stung (perhaps it was?) and thundered after Anna's. Mine accepted the challenge, his trot changed into a smooth gallop, his ears flattened, his neck stretched out. The race was on! So we sped by the colossus of Memanon with less than a glance, our faculties directed solely to self-preservation. That night we were too tired to speak. Anna stayed in bed the whole next day, then supposing Luxor had no comparable adventure to offer, decided to return to Cairo. I said I was going to the Sudan. Neither really believed the other until we parted at the station, on opposite platforms.

It was cooler in the station master's office and there were fewer flies. I waited there listening to the bargaining techniques of the station master and a Sudanese involved in the buying and selling of a chicken. Often sure that I would get no further on a trip, I developed my interest in, and my awareness of, my immediate surroundings to help pass the time. The train was an hour late, during this delay they prolonged their performance. At the end only the bird looked wilted.

A thin strip of deck of the paddle steamer separated my cabin from the railings and the Nile. I lay on my bed watching the sunrise through the open door. On either shore rocky mountains jutted out of sand. 'It is Nubia,' the steward, with a grimace, dismissed this land that held no sign of life as far as I could see. A man from the next cabin later kindly lent me his binoculars. Through them I noticed to my surprise many different animal footprints leading to the water's edge. This once fertile valley had been flooded by the building of the

Aswan dam, he said. I had not understood what the tops of palm trees were doing in the water. My neighbour pointed out a half-submerged temple. For hours we glided down the yellow-green river. Around a bend the temple of Abu Simbel appeared, its facade carved into a cliff, its entrance still on a bit of dry ground. One tree grew there and to it our paddle steamer was tied. Soon all this would be lost. The giant statues of the Pharaoh might be removed to high ground, my fellow-passenger, who turned out to be an Oxford-educated Syrian, explained. Another scheme to save the site from inundation involved a plastic bubble. If acquired, the vast amount of money needed for either plan should be spent on helping the poor of the region, not protecting a temple, I thought.

Thanks to the Syrian's torch we could see traces of the original paint inside the temple's dark halls. We studied the spirited reliefs recording the Pharaoh's campaigns and conquests. Travelling alone did not worry me again after that day.

Again a locust tree provided our mooring at the town of Wadi Halfa in the Sudan. The other passengers would continue their journey to Khartoum by train. Before he left the Syrian helped me choose a hotel, or rather I chose it and he called it, 'Native and unsuitable.' I loved my spacious room where swallows had a nest in the corner and the parent birds swooped back and forth through the open window to feed their young. My bed, a four poster, was painted with roses. The clean pink blankets, the raw wood floor scrubbed white and a water jug, a masterpiece of spontaneous throwing, added to its charm. My wellington boots, so useful in Italy, I put under my bed and left there.

For breakfast I made coffee on my cup, with solid fuel, an Italian 'stove'; at midday I ate sandwiches and fruit, for dinner I went to the Nile Hotel. The hotel guests were curious about me though more curious about a girl who came to the dining room draped in a leopard skin, her face and body crimson from sun-bathing. Two ladies at my table awaiting the next train, hearing I would stay a few days, asked, 'But what will you *do*?' The Syrian, parting from me, had used the same phrase.

The police offered me a camel as soon as I went out the first

21

morning. It lay down for me to get on and then got up, one end at a time, in the reverse order expected. I found myself far from the ground with an aching bruise in my back and another in my stomach from the high-sided saddle. The animal turned its head backwards and made threatening noises when a whip was handed to me, so instead of a carefree gallop we walked, a policeman accompanying me, to a near-by village. A girl, bare-shouldered, short-skirted, cigarette hanging from her mouth, I suppose the local prostitute, came out to greet me but the greeting turned to raucous laughter when, with hands on hips, she watched my awkwardness on camel back. She implied she would curse me unless I gave her money. Infuriated by her rudeness to a guest, the policeman jumped off his camel and chased her waving his truncheon. Respectable women of the village were busy plaiting dry grass into strips to be sewn together for baskets or mats, another unenviable occupation. From the top of the camel I could see that the high surrounding walls of each house protected a private oasis of plants, water jugs and shade. Outside, wandering flocks of goats ate the garbage and also every growing thing. We circled a mosque and then returned on a road built by the British 'when they were after Rommel'. Visions of trees and their reflections in lakes so perfect, I could not believe were mirages until we rode through them.

A famous crocodile hunter we met invited me to tea. Heads of the victims on stakes surrounded his mud-brick house. 'For you British,' he served tea with milk (normally it had only sugar) and showed me a medal, 'From Queen Victoria', earned by his grandfather for guiding boats over the cataracts. As a memento he presented me with a crocodile head. It was an interesting afternoon though I would have enjoyed social encounters more if each had not involved the ordeal of raising and lowering the camel. I had not yet got it right and thought again of poor Anna.

At sunset the desert changed colours until the sky became black and the stars bright. A vivid spectrum outlined the rim of the earth. Sharp rocky hills divided valleys of sand down which we rode. In one place fallen tree trunks blocked our homeward path. I got off and touched them and found they were cold, immovable, stone, petrified.

Though I persevered with the camel, the cook's offer to lend me his donkey was a blessing and I returned the 'best, white, racing camel'. Now I could scoot around on this, according to the police, déclassé form of transport. I went to the Wadi Halfa museum, a good art exhibition at the government school for boys, the hospital and visited the D.C. On one trip I met Mrs Hamilton, an American woman employed by the United Nations, in what capacity, I could not guess. From the Nile Hotel she rode forth on a camel in a fluttering silk dress, a knotted handkerchief on her head. She braved dismounting for a single photograph. 'One of the first rules of travel I learned was to wear an ample skirt which lets one move! You can never tell what is going to happen next.' Mrs Hamilton at fifty-five had been everywhere. On her return from each foreign trip she gave lectures illustrated with colour slides. Again I visited museums, schools, hospitals in her company, noticing how she stunned officials with a barrage of questions, pencil and notebook ready even on camel back. 'I want to see *people,*' she exclaimed, 'I want to learn about what I see.' In her opinion most tourists wasted their time. When Mrs Hamilton visited South America she gave up modern transport to cross some remote wilderness on a donkey. Finally the animal wore out, then the guide collapsed, only when there was no alternative did she charter an aeroplane.

I was invited to a farewell luncheon given for Mrs Hamilton by the Sudanese government. It took place in an official's home furnished with lots of brass trays, six stuffed leopards and fine carpets. The meal of a freshly slaughtered sheep, specially prepared rice, piles of vegetables and four sweets was served dish by dish and, thinking each course was the last, we helped ourselves heartily. Finally servants poured water from silver jugs over our hands. For Mrs Hamilton it had been an event worth the effort of sitting cross-legged for two hours. I still preferred finding the petrified trees.

We returned together from Wadi Halfa to Aswan by steamer. On deck one evening she found me stamping on a scorpion and tried to convince me of its 'news value to the folks back home'. In the confined space of my cabin the crocodile head smelt unpleasant and was only bad news as far as I could judge. I pushed it far under my bunk. Before I got away, however, a faithful steward rushed after me brandishing the head. Once more, leaving it behind on the train, I was almost safely out of Luxor station when an honest porter clutching the great yellow-toothed artifact caught up with me. I had bronchitis and had decided to return to Luxor for a rest while Mrs Hamilton was whisked away in the night by *Wagon Lit Cook*, first class, to Cairo.

The first morning of my return I had a slight fever and fell asleep in the public gardens. The town snake charmer was sitting beside me when I awoke. Uninvited he selected a snake from his padded basket and placed it before us on the grass. Without musical accompaniment the show was a dull one and his having to smack the snake into action made it sadder still. The young man's father had been employed for a Cecil B. de Mille movie, then, after being bitten, had died. I asked where the boy found the snakes. He heard 'the word of God', yes, in a dream, telling him where to catch them. He smiled a brilliant smile of certainty and that is the look I remember, the expression my camera missed when I took his photograph.

Donkeys left at the entrance of the dark post office put their heads around the door and watched their masters. On the floor two scribes sat cross-legged waiting for letters to be dictated. The postman, mouth agape, fumbled through sheets of stamps with thick fingers while staring at people pushing for a place at the counter. I was allowed to help myself from the *Poste Restante* shelf where alphabetical order, any order, was non-existent. 'Please forward or backward' were the instruction on one of my letters which I took to read in the park. Gardeners watering the grass were asleep and oblivious of the fact that half the lawn had turned into a lake. One side of the garden was bordered by jewellers' shops selling silver ankle bangles and antique shops indicated by stuffed crocodiles hung above their doors. 'Antiques' was a label of the town's more exclusive days. Now a plane brought in a hundred sightseers from Rome or Tokyo each week, many of whom just wanted a souvenir to prove they had been to Upper Egypt.

Luxor had few dramas. Today's started with a runaway horse, then came a funeral winding through town to the mosque. Musicians preceding the procession made a melancholy noise on drum and trumpet. The pink-nosed stallion leading was impatient at having to walk so slowly and tossed his head at every step. The mosque, only a few hundred years old and built in the ruins of the ancient Egyptian temple of Luxor was, since the temple's excavation in the nineteenth century, left on a mound in the middle. Undoubtedly, the townspeople considered their mosques to be infinitely more important, though compared in size to the temple, it was the flea in the elephant's ear.

This time I crossed the Nile and walked to the Theban cliffs alone. Again the desolate land with limpid air intrigued me. At last in the vivid personal paintings of the nobles' tombs I found an aspect of Egyptian art that spoke to me. One noble had depicted in his funerary chamber his happiest moments with mobile figures and intimate detail (the cat of Nakht sits eating under his chair), while the pharaohs had the sun god or Osiris, king of the underworld, portrayed in formal religious scenes on *their* tombs. I moved along the walls fascinated by the picture of daily life here. Light came from a mirror which the guard held reflecting sunlight into each tomb room. The guard, despondent from the start, was slow to follow me with light. I coughed, I clapped my hands and shouted. There was no response. I went outside to find him lying on the ground, writhing and groaning in the agony of toothache. Nothing could be done. I gave up and returned to the ferry. Aspirin was another item I always carried after that.

Children begging for money and following me everywhere were a problem, then I learned their names and told them to call me 'Fatima'. Miraculously the situation changed; they would greet me and rush off to annoy another tourist. 'Fatima,' a voice would say, a dark face would smile shyly in the market or main street. Once I hired a taxi and took as many as would fit in for a drive around the garden. They went nearly mad with excitement. I was too poor to do more. It was just as well, there were too many children.

During Ramadan at dawn a cannon signalled the start of the Moslem fast and once more at sunset to mark its ending. Children gathered each evening and holding their hands over their ears, half in terror, half in joyful anticipation, danced around me in a frenzy suggesting a massacre was more likely than the firing of a single shot. That month the Ramadan bang was my morning alarm; it had to be loud enough to be heard throughout the town.

'Fatima' I may have been to my neighbours, at the boarding house I was 'Miss English', for that is what Metwalli the concierge called me. Metwalli was shiny black with an infectious giggle and a squashed flat nose, a contrast to the high-arched nose of his assistant Ali. Ali, a fanatical Moslem, gave the impression that it was beneath him to say more than 'Good morning'. Actually his English was limited. Usually he would be fervently reading the Koran aloud or praying on the floor so instead of asking for the key or help in lighting the fire, I'd flee until Metwalli returned. Metwalli's gown was simply a floor-length shirt. Ali wore a white turban, traditional dress with flared skirt and sleeves. Several times a week Ali walked to his home in Karnak for fresh laundry. Although very poor he was extremely proud of his family. Did he realise he resembled exactly the decadent-looking Aknaton, one of the principal builders of Karnak's temple? Metwalli, on the other hand, had no family. He came from Nubia, it was said scornfully.

In the evening we sat on the balcony overlooking the street. Metwalli entertained me by summarizing the character of each passer-by. 'The Supreme' would be the chief of police. 'The Betrayer' a shop-keeper who sold sugar short in weight. Metwalli enjoyed himself. Ali, after his prayers, stood in the corner leaning against the wall, staring out blankly.

Four tourists from the boarding house invited me to join them on a trip to Banana Island. My share of hiring the boat and three crew would be ninepence, a sum I could just afford out of my by then half a crown a day budget. No breeze disturbed the Nile when we set out. One of the Arab crew punted, another in a canvas harness walked along the bank towing. We had brought bread, cheese and fruit. The Arab who punted made us tea on his stove and broke the Ramadan fast by eating with us, which disgusted the older man at the tiller. Our triangular sails were reflected in the shiny river and the scenery glided past. Banana Island, we found, had not only bananas, it had mangoes, oranges, sugar cane and dates growing there. We returned to the boat with more fruit to the dismay of the tiller man who regarded food as further temptation to his men. We sunbathed farther up the Nile and then floating, let the strong current carry us back to the mooring. The boat men decribed the Nile's hazards, such as whirlpools and worms that ate one's liver (explained by particularly vivid mime). The American couple with us, mistaking the big lizards on the shore for crocodiles, wouldn't swim anyhow. That afternoon the current took us back to Luxor twice as quickly as we had come and the sail made pleasant shade. Everyone sang, including the crew when they weren't trying to sell us a cruise to Cairo that would take weeks.

I began to enjoy bargaining. Indifference was the most important factor I learned accidentally when a souvenir seller showed me 'A genuine antique. (I am not a liar! I am not a liar!), for a pound and a half.'

I said, 'No thank you.'

Then he tried, 'Because you are British, price one pound.' I looked uninterested. He thought again. 'You student, not tourist, seventy-five piastres.' I told him to go. He answered, 'You are my friend, twenty-five piastres.' Finally, as I was leaving, the object, a crudely carved stone sphinx was offered to ten piastres with the remark, 'welcome'. I wish I had bought it. The weight of carrying it in my rucksack and lack of money had put me off getting it at the beginning, fortunately. I had learnt a lesson.

'A fairly well-known archaeologist,' as the English man described himself, arrived in Luxor. He had a shrill laugh, affected manners and knew every important site in Europe and the Middle East, not to mention all the right people. He had set out in a jeep for remote Saint Catherine's monastery in Sinai, got lost, run out of petrol, and finally reached it. 'What have *you* done?' He asked.

'Nothing much,' I admitted. This ruthless hunting of monuments depressed me though perhaps I should have appreciated his knowledge. To 'Mr English', the name Metwalli gave him, Egyptians and the scenery were, for the most part, invisible. The Englishman lectured me on the antiquities of Thebes. 'How often do you go?'

'Oh, I'm going again soon.' I did not want to make a date

with him. The evening was balmy, he took my arm and walked me along the promenade to the brightly lit postcard shop. One of the proprietors came forward and sanctimoniously kissed my hand. 'Last week Mussolini's daughter was here. This week I meet you!' he cried. Mr English giggled as we were given bright green imitation scarabs. 'I like wars, monsieur,' the shop owner was saying, 'they are very good for business....' Unnoticed I slipped away, Metwalli was expecting me.

At the end of Ramadan Metwalli had his one holiday of the year. He would go out on the river boat with his friends. I told him not to worry, I would look after the building. He and the others set sail, packed tight on the crowded deck, singing, while I waved from the roof. It was hot. One part of the flat roof used as a refuse dump would make an ideal place for sunbathing if I burnt the rubbish. I got some matches and at once the dump blazed. It roared. the mud-brick of the walls burned black. Metwalli, out on the Nile on his only holiday saw the building apparently in flames. I guessed with a sick, sinking faintness that the fire was likely to burn through the floor. Footsteps fluttered up the stairs. It was Ali who we thought was in Karnak. In a minute he reappeared with a bucket of water, turban and robe discarded. Silently, again and again he came back, carrying bucket after bucket until the flames were extinguished. I tried to help; he motioned me away. Ali looked at me with a smile, the first look or smile he had given me.

Well, I was not allowed to forget the fire, it was Metwalli's joke which made him nearly burst with giggles every day for the rest of my stay. 'Miss English. Fire on roof!' was enough to set him off in convulsions of laughter. I joined in and we both staggered about clutching our stomachs in the agony of laughing so much. A faint smile would haunt Ali's extraordinary features and from then on Ali sat with us on the balcony and we three watched the strolling crowd every evening.

A high spiral of hawks drifted around the sky except when an eagle crossed on its way to the cliffs. Then the smaller birds evaporated in its path. How violent, still and monotonous Egypt was. The blue, green and yellow day-time landscape with black figures seldom varied. I sat on the roof as the sun set and the sky turned shades of pink, yellow and pale blue. Silhouettes of palms grew a wonderful raw black while the last orange rays of sun were snuffed out in purple darkness. The minarets of Luxor, draped with small electric lights made me think of Christmas trees and sailboats' reflections, even at night, of open white butterflies drifting in silence on the current. Why did I stay so long? It was not for sunsets, I had recovered from bronchitis. Was it laziness or loneliness or had the stillness of Egyptian life captivated me? When I had to return to England I was glad, relieved even at the thought of working again. Isn't that the way one should return from a holiday?

No lights functioned on the evening train to Cairo. At stations I could see only the whites of people's eyes. Because of everyone's chewing sugar cane the floor was as ankle deep in fodder as a cattle-truck. All night fine sand blew through the 3rd class carriages' wide open windows. I covered myself completely with a blanket, like the others, and slept. I could not expect anonymity here but a night of it was restful. In Cairo a sandstorm raged. Such were the clouds of dust in Station Square it might have been the desert except that out of the blowing sand would come a woman trying to sell a duck or the frightening sound of an invisible car. The filth of Egypt could be accepted, not the sandstorms; they were unbearable because they had to be shared.

Metwalli's last act, as I left, was to place the stinking crocodile head on top of my rucksack. Then I had a brainwave. It would be a gift for the hotel manager's son in Cairo. The little boy was thrilled and the manager, accepting my thoughtfulness as an indirect compliment, supervised the DDT-ing of my room. He recommended a good cheap restaurant and shouted at the proprietor which resulted in a flurry of service while I ate; the waiters conscientiously flicked their cloths not at the flies but at the starving cats under tables and behind chairs.

Now I viewed the old sphinx with warm familiarity. I went back to the pyramids to examine the well-fitting blocks, climbing up even a couple of them was enough to give me vertigo. On a camel, my father had visited them years earlier and we had reached the same conclusion: that here was one of the wonders of the world. At least getting to the pyramids was an adventure about which I could boast to my friends. Trying to impress them was synonymous with trying to be happy. I thought that's all that was needed.

Anna had complained about the Egyptian museum being hopelessly full and badly arranged. Admittedly mummies were piled to the ceiling in some places and rare descriptive labels in English often placed upside down. Had Tutankhamen worn his sandals of solid gold? Photographs I had seen gave no idea of the actual richness of these treasures. The Islamic museum owned the finest and most fantastic collection of early ceramic lustre bowls. The Modern museum had a Hieronymous Bosch. And in the library I read that Islam asks us to find joy and comfort not only with God, also with the people in whom He is. The Koran stressed the fact that we could choose, at any moment, by our actions, the heaven or hell on earth in which we would live.

The manager allowed me to sit on the hotel's flat roof from where workmen were suspended, hanging over the side painting an Arab name instead of the former 'The Hotel France'. In the square below almost everyone was selling bananas. A priest carrying a white parasol glanced at the only woman selling oranges. A little boy, finding a stone that marked, drew a hopscotch design. The banana seller chased him away. I could see the next picture drawn by the child was a person, he kept banging the stone on the face making extra eyes. Then he sat cross-legged and looked back at the old man banana seller who looked away. It must have been his mother who had left him in charge on the straw behind her crate of oranges. He decided to eat one. He sang. No one bought from him. He sat in the straw nest like a little bird with a long neck watching everyone. He sneaked another orange out of the crate and slipped pieces of it into his mouth by pretending to rub his nose. A child of about five came along. The boy behind the oranges offered him one. The younger child pointed to a larger orange. The old man with the bananas saw and shouted. That ended it. The woman had returned the next time I looked. She held her head in her hands. A dealer with a large push-cart of oranges must have been doing all the business. He took care to arrange his fruit in pyramids, he knew each orange, each had its place. Even when weighing out some for a customer he was right the first time.

Dilapidated horse cabs rolled by, the horses' ribs as clear as the spokes of the wheels. At least our neighbours' were better fed. From the funeral parlour next to the hotel a groom brought out four, then a white and gold hearse. The man climbed on top to put a wooden angel in place. He led out six more horses. The orange lady was eating her own fruit and watching listlessly. Next came a baby's coffin. All the groom's trappings had to be removed from the hearse before it went in. There was a terrific to-do hitching up ten horses. The old banana man paid no attention even when they drove away. He stroked his bananas as if making them into smooth bunches of his own design. He had a white beard and an infinite variety of ways of squatting in a tiny space.

Another funeral was being prepared outside the hotel. Eight horses swished their tails and tossed their heads trying to avoid the obligatory ear hoods and black blankets. A groom placed a wreath of purple and yellow paper flowers on the front and then the golden cross on top. This hearse was gilded, with cherubim. Anna had thought it, 'Like the carriage your Queen rides in.' One groom threaded the reins, another slid a dish of baked beans out of the still empty hearse and ate. The four grooms put on white smocks over their dirty ones, then red fezes, though they wore no shoes. The street cleaner waited in case there was a job for him. Taking turns, the grooms tied their red cummerbunds to the wheel and then wrapped themselves up before squatting together on the kerb to share the last of the beans. The horses rubbed each other in an effort to get off their black hoods. A strong breeze ruffled the paper flowers. Children made noises at the eight horses hoping to start them though it was the children who dashed away when a groom stood to jab the horses and make them stand straight. The driver arrived at last. He was handed the reins. A whip cracked and cracked. They all went. Only the street cleaner's basket remained, he was sweeping his way around the square hardly looking at what he did. The wind blew bits of paper over his long twig broom.

The simplicity of my life made it insignificant but I knew all I saw was a microcosm of the whole world and that I could learn as much from my life, if I thought about it, as I could from lots of books. Oh dear, already I sound like Mrs Hamilton. The United Nations is sending her to Syria, a country she recommends. That is where I will go on my next holiday.

Saved

Since dawn our bus to Baghdad had been stuck in the desert between Syria and Iraq where continuous rain turned the sand into a sea of mud. That evening, in the hope a light would attract attention, we burnt petrol-soaked rags but no one came to our rescue.

A Lebanese boy on his way to work in Kuwait shared his bag of sunflower seeds. We cracked and spat out the fine shell before eating the minute kernel. Passengers, predominantly merchants from Baghdad and Damascus, took turns providing a cigarette for the driver, a tall woolly-headed Arab who told me his life-story with the help of an Iraqi interpreter. The story consisted of five years in the army, five years in prison, seven years with motor cars (he demonstrated this by pretending to drive our stationary bus). Presumably he was in prison for knifing; he made a throat-cutting gesture.

A fat Syrian *commerçant* for a troupe of dancing girls came to the front of the bus saying how urgent it was that he reach Baghdad, and that the driver was terrible. The driver gesticulated wildly, he moaned, huge tears rolled down his cheeks. What else could he do? Nothing marked the frontiers, neither was there a road in this limitless desert spotted with camels. Darkness fell. We gave up thinking and awaited our fate.

Interminable dawn, cold, overcast sky; we opened our eyes to another day the same as the last. Holding up their robes, wading through mud, passengers gathered prickly plants to put under the wheels. It was useless. The bus had sunk too far. We pushed and slipped and cried, 'Allah!' The bus moved forward a centimetre at a time. Who considered the hundreds of kilometres left to Baghdad?

When I had to go to the loo all the men, scrupulously polite, looked away which made our being stranded not such an unpleasant experience for me, just a trying one we shared equally. Despite our being able to wash our feet in the water supply all desert buses carry, mud covered everything. Only the fat Syrian stayed immaculate in the back seat, a wide-brimmed hat stuck firmly on his head, a briefcase clasped against his round stomach.

Before the second night grew dark two Bedouin with old faces, bare-footed, wrapped in sheepskins, came from nowhere to watch us. Snowflakes drifted through the black sky. We could no longer even push the bus, an axle had broken and two tyres were punctured.

At noon on the third day we were saved. Police out on a hunting trip came across us accidentally. Their ankle-length sheepskin coats and red and white *keffyehs* hiding all but their eyes made them look wonderful. The officer handed me a piece of chocolate and lent me his fur-lined gloves and I felt warmth gradually come back to the rest of my body. With ease their jeeps tore across the sodden sand to the police post. I was given a cement cell to myself. The male passengers who were ferried also, later shared the common room.

A fox the officer had shot during the trip he hung on the clothes' hook. He brought me a glass of tea and pointed to a bottle of brandy under the bed, saying, 'For it is very cold here in winter.' His English was fairly good except when he asked me to, 'Come and see the twilight.' He meant 'toilet'. Offered a 'bath' I imagined soaking in a hot tub for hours. A bowl of boiling water was brought in, that was it.

I slept, unconscious from the moment I laid down until they woke me for a breakfast of warm ewe's milk and dates. My refusing a glass of whisky with the chief of police caused him to doubt my nationality. 'All English drink,' he announced with the authority of his rank.

Another bus materialized. The rest of the way was dry and well marked. We stopped at a *chicana*, a desert café, and ordered enormous bowls of rice for lunch. The Syrian *commerçant* wolfed his food, his gold teeth flashing as he chewed open-mouthed. Speaking in French he asked if I would like a job though I had told him I could not dance.

Suspicious, I asked the reason, 'You make everyone feel at ease with you,' he observed. I wondered how much dancing his girls did.

I loved Baghdad. What better way was there to spend the winter than sunbathing on the hotel roof? *The Times* (only a week old) showed photographs of tourists in St Moritz. I had had enough snow! After last winter's ski-ing in Arosa, my only recollection was of feeling fit. Baghdad's dustiness might become stifling later on, even now the Tigris was an unromantic mud colour, but the place gave me a completely fresh outlook and that was my idea of a good holiday. My three weeks' ski-ing had cost the same as two months here.

My hotel was on Rachid Street, an arcaded thoroughfare of character, and at the hotel entrance awaited ever available chickens tied in big bunches. An old woman sat among them, among the wings opening and closing like fans around her; her eyes beseeched me to buy. The sound of the hens' gentle clucking seemed to infiltrate every room and remind me of her.

The souk fascinated me. I spent days exploring the labyrinth of festooned passages. Copper, silk, spices, furs, pottery or paper, each was sold in its own section. If I asked the way from a turbaned cross-legged merchant I would be offered tea. If I admired the souk, I was told it would be pulled down soon because it was 'old'. If I objected – to anything, I was classified as another eccentric English woman, a type they knew well, that usually made a bee-line for Baghdad, and whom they took politely in their stride.

Curiously, the Mesopotamian art of four thousand years ago meant more to me than any other. The faces' primitive, strange look made me study each piece with concern while the perfection of Greek and Roman statues I accepted at a glance. Here was the source, I felt.

The police officer who had rescued us in the desert telephoned his brother-in-law, a doctor in Baghdad, and asked him to reserve a hotel room for me. When a strange man drove up and said, 'You are coming with me,' as I stepped off the bus, I did not know this, nor who he was. I walked in the other direction. Convincing me that he was genuinely friendly took some time.

The following day he invited me to lunch at his house and on arrival I had a preview of the feast as the sheep's throat had just been cut and I had to step over a pool of blood to enter. Women were stirring a vat of soup in the courtyard and cats surreptitiously licked the bowls. I was hurried to the privacy of a small room crowded with plush-covered furniture. On the table a plastic coronation cloth showed the profiles of Elizabeth and Philip. Eventually such quantities of food arrived two more tables were needed. Only the doctor and his male relatives ate with me. The doctor's wife, sisters, mother and daughters who would eat what we left, peered through curtains dividing our room from theirs.

After the meal I questioned the doctor about his work. His eyes were foxy, his nose bulbous, his hair frizzy, his manner direct. 'The people are ill,' he began, 'that child has worms.' He pointed to a little boy crawling across the carpet. 'And I have piles and chronic appendicitis and no holiday so how can I take time to cure myself?' I praised the excellent lunch. He retorted that people did not understand food's nutritional value or the benefits of cleanliness. 'For instance,' he went on, 'my father lives in this crowded house. He has enough money to build a better house outside Baghdad but he asks why should he change when he was born here.' The doctor's words were interrupted by the cock-a-doodle-do of a rooster that had got into the room. The bird infuriated him. His expression was bitter. 'We were two years with the British but my wife could not acclimatize herself. It was impossible. I had the choice of divorcing, and it is very easy with our religion,' he brushed his hands together three times, 'or returning here.' The doctor considered marriage lacked companionship especially among the lower classes. 'Young girls can speak to no one before they are married, afterwards they have every freedom. As a doctor I have learned many secrets which could ruin families. It is the reverse of your European system, and that is a pity.' His greatest wish was that his children be educated in the West. Before answering some of my questions he hesitated. 'I don't know if I can trust you; if this goes any further, I will be in prison tomorrow, believe me.' Gradually, I heard that he judged the government to be utterly corrupt, that the two per cent who ruled bought their positions and power. 'Yes, the British leave, they leave pro-British Iraqis in their place. I could not be a Communist and the majority of the people could not be either, for they are too religious, but the government, in order to control our protests, call us 'Communists' and put us in prison. It will be seven or eight years maybe .... Then ....' He begged, 'Please don't be angry but ninety-eight per cent hate the British, that's only topped by 100 per cent who hate the Jews. You asked to hear the truth. I have probably done wrong to tell you what I know.'

'I am English. I have Jewish friends. How can you trust me?' I inquired.

'*Boy* friends?' he wanted to know.

'*Good* friends.'

'Well, you are different, you come here as our *guest.*'

'And what sort of government do you want?'

'A pro-Iraqi government!' The doctor smiled at last.

One day, when he had to visit patients in the area, the doctor took me to Babylon. Outside Baghdad the dry earth plain stretched as far as one could see. Slouching camels walked by parked aeroplanes at the airport, cloud-like masses were far away flocks of sheep. New cars, smashed and twisted, lay beside the road. An eagle tore up a dead dog. Packed station-wagons decorated with feather dusters and flags roared towards town. Among the acres of date-palms, the villages were deceptively idyllic. Only when we stopped for tea did I notice the children were dirty, the donkeys had sores, and flies crawled over our food.

Babylon was the mound at the end of a dirt track, three hours drive south of Baghdad. The guide described the sunken brick-lined passages, 'This is Procession Street,' he said, and we walked beside remains of the Istar Temple or the palace of Nebuchadnezzar, names he rattled off without explanation. Piles of mud-bricks looked the same to me then. On a wall glazed monsters, cast in relief, might have inspired the ceramic advertisements in the Paris metro. The guide showed us a column marking the place where the code of laws was found, but he talked more about a stork's nest built on top of it. 'The Hanging Gardens!' he cried as if to stimulate our imagination; there was little to be seen and no more was said on the subject. That tour introduced me to my ignorance.

To the north of Baghdad, on another visit, the doctor pointed out the gold-domed mosque, the holy shrine of Kadhmain. Hre told me about the two sects of Moslems: the Sinas (the most numerous) and the Shias (mainly Persian in origin). The Shias had formed a community in Kadhmain and built the mosque. Being an infidel, I was not allowed inside so after peering through the gates of the courtyard, we went to a nearby restaurant for kebab, a beef dish made everywhere in Iraq but made best in Kadhmain, the doctor claimed.

The police officer, on leave, came to Baghdad to see me. He no longer looked dashing and I no longer needed saving. He had thought of me often in his lonely out-post, he said. Perhaps there wasn't much else? He invited me to a movie and I made the mistake of accepting. That morning a letter informed me my godmother (whom I had never met) had left me a hundred pounds in her will, and I would have shared the good news had he not drawn a revolver to shoot a fly on the ceiling during the interval. Such a juvenile action annoyed me. On impulse I announced I was leaving the country. I felt certain my godmother would have liked me to use her money for travel. Why not India, I thought. It seemed a marvellous idea to go as far as possible and see as much as I could.

* * *

The sun had set and everyone prayed on tattered carpets in the Baghdad station. One man remained grilling meat: fanning the charcoal, making sparks fly. Dogs waiting at a distance from the food-stall showed their intense anticipation in the way their shoulders moved as they shifted, crouched and sat again.

With a long, 'Whoo-whoo, whoo,' the train pulled out of Baghdad. Stars shone, moonlight was bright on the earth. A 'psychology man' read my palm, predicting everyone would treat me kindly, that I would have peace on my travels and the man I married would be the only one I loved. I would live to be eighty-one, he assured me. 'Chi. Chi. Chi,' the procession of boys selling tea ended with the smallest in charge of the washing-up bucket. All seats were filled, the aisles also. An Arab who had standing space by the door fingered his prayer beads, silent and still; he knew how to travel.

The policemen in whose protection I had been placed, found a new interest having caught a couple of boys without tickets. The police plonked them down on the floor by my feet. Patiently the prisoners held out their big floppy hands until the handcuffs could be made to work. After locking them together, the police moved their rifles and leaned back in their seats reflectively. We three were scrutinized through half-closed eyes. The boys, who wore torn jackets and white cloths twisted untidily around their heads, sat close, while one licked a cigarette-paper and the other, despite handcuffs, helped roll it. One of the policemen changed into a brown night-shirt, wrapped a woollen scarf around his head and climbing into the luggage-rack to sleep, accidentally kicked a soldier. The two argued. It is only sixteen hours to Basrah, I thought, and kept my eyes closed for a long time. When I opened them there was a red slit at the horizon and an apathetic light revealing nothing but desert. The sun rose quickly. It was blinding. 'Chi! Chi! Chi!' cried the teamakers. In the middle of the carriage a big kettle boiled on a primus stove. I was passed a sticky glassful by the policeman who had lent me his blanket. He managed to ask me where I was going. When I replied, 'India,' they pointed to one of the passengers. I guessed he was an Indian. They were delighted because he got up and bowed.

* * *

Face to face with it my 'India' was a vast, terrifying, mysterious, plague-ridden country and I felt frightened as I stepped ashore, alone in Bombay. Timidly, I asked the way to an hotel from an official who spoke English. He pointed to a red London bus that went straight to the hotel's door. Indians were playing cricket in the park, the sun shone on flowering trees, and my mood changed: why hadn't I come here sooner?

The big ugly hotel was not far from the sea and though 'tea-time' was over, I was served. The white bread smelt of mildew or moth balls, distinct even under the jelly-jam. Potted plants along the hotel verandah, supposed to hide

39

guests, revealed hungry children staring through and holding out their hands. The receptionist came by, 'What are you doing, dear? Writing letters? That's good, dear.' She looked over my shoulder, 'You happy here, dear? There's more of a breeze at the other corner, you know.' One did not need to answer.

A Burmese lady in the room next to mine wore pinafore saris and had a face like a Gauguin. She and her friend had come to Bombay for a holiday and they gambled from morning to night, I could hear the cards being shuffled through the thin wall. She exclaimed, when I asked if they were enjoying their visit, 'Oh, we would be happy in the jungle!' Spliced bamboo curtains allowed a diluted combination of sun and shade into my room. From the balcony I looked out on coconut palms taller than the buildings, flame coloured flowers, and a shimmering sea between the houses. Only when they flew were the green parrots distinguishable from the foliage: the whole garden was an aviary. Electric lights came on as the sky turned pale lavender A typewriter pattered, someone called, 'Elsie, Elsie,' in a pseudo-English way. A passing *ghari* was pulled by a piebald horse so strongly marked that one forgot the night's light and shadows. I knew already India would be the most beautiful Eastern country I had seen, and also it would be the one to hold my interest least, because of its Englishness, perhaps.

An officer from the ship on which I had travelled down the Gulf invited me out to dinner. Though he asked me where I wanted to go and what I wanted to eat, he obviously always went to the same restaurant and ate the 'safe' food. He implied it would be very unwise to do differently. The officer had a fragile physique, pleasant blue eyes, and teeth, not really prominent, just on a larger scale than the rest of him. Among his fellow officers who constantly discussed the two Ss (Ship and Sex) he felt lonely. Once he had been seduced, he admitted. The night before his friends had made him paint a sign on a rival ship saying 'For Sale', and now he was tortured by guilt. Before dinner we walked in a park where I was so thrilled to see grass again that I jumped the railings and ran across it. 'Please! Let's be British,' he admonished me. In the returning taxi he tried to kiss me. He was easily discouraged, that too, one felt, was only part of a routine.

The silent, massive street crowd dressed mostly in white walked in the shade of their open black umbrellas. Some beggars had only heads and bodies, if they had limbs, the limbs were likely to be swollen by elephantiasis. As for performing bears, monkeys and mongooses, the pavement was alive with them. I leaned against low railings of an enclosure to watch stray animals being fed by a sect who believed so devoutly in the sanctity of life they even tried to avoid stepping on ants. As I turned, I noticed my clothes adhering firmly to the rail. It had been freshly painted. With a limited wardrobe this was a disaster. Disaster? I looked again at the people who couldn't walk, who couldn't see, and those who hadn't enough to eat.

In Bombay's streets advertising was plastered on every available space. Useful shops around the hotel were 'The Edward VIII Ice Cream and Fish Dishes', 'The Rembrandt and Van Dyck Ltd. Photographers', 'The Book Shop, Browse In' and 'The Tibetan Curious Shop'. One small shop's sign advised, 'Palmist. Not to Worry But Visit Hurry'.

* * *

Signs in the Bombay station were of the same design and colour as those in the London Underground. 'Whisky. Biscuits. Biscuits. Whisky', the platform salesman loitered and repeated his message for my benefit; there was prohibition for natives. The porters' red shirts had faded to different shades of pink or terracotta, on turbaned heads they carried the train-passengers' brass pots and bedding rolls. Pigeons' wings clapped together in sudden flight at our departure and we slowly passed waving people on the platform, then a lot of corrugated iron shacks from which people didn't wave. Round baskets were being carried over a bridge, above the crush of the crowd the baskets were held up like sun-nets. Even the mixture of banyan trees, flowering magnolias and men in topis was almost a familiar sight. 'Curry Road' one was called. At a crossing I met a bullock's stoic gaze and watched Parsee children waving bunches of orange blossom entwined with tinsel, and calling, 'Goodbye, goodbye.'

41

Opposite me, in the carriage, an Indian girl slipped off her sandals, folded her legs underneath her and passed me *The Gospel According to St John*. Many words were heavily underlined in red. She was astonished when I said, 'No thank you.' She began reading it herself. Her concentration was none too good. She confided that this was her first trip alone and that we were on the Poona express. I did know where I was going but I didn't tell her I had no other plans: all I was sure of was meeting the right people at the right time. The Indian girl was a maid going to an English couple in Poona and she took me along. Being missionaries, this young couple, the Browns, immediately offered help by settling me in a hostel and showing me where to hire a bicycle, all I needed, I assured them.

A large stone-floored dining hall, high-backed chairs at the long table, and the starkness of the rooms, made the hostel rather medieval. The matron, an old English woman, her white hair in a bun, spoke only to pronounce grace. Hostilities existed between Afro-Indians and Anglo-Indians. One of them, pointing to a couple of girls in saris who looked no different from the rest, hissed, "*They're* Jewish!' The Christian girls asked me endless questions about the Royal family and proved capable of discussing Princess Margaret for a whole hour.

If there were an argument the English woman muttered, 'Poor things,' She owned an old tom-cat to whom she talked despite his hiding in the bushes between feeding times. She interrupted her search for him one morning to tell me she had lived here sixty-two years. 'I don't even know the other side of Poona, only this side, the veterinary hospital, the officers' mess. We used to go there to hear the brass band. Yes, I came here as a schoolgirl . . . .'

The high front hedge was covered with purple morning-glories, their vines climbed into the trees. Over red and yellow nasturtiums, butterflies fluttered in a cloud. Coconut palms with stiff fronds, swayed and shone in the sun. Weeds hid cherubs supporting a bird-bath, a broken arch for roses was now being held in place by the thick plant. Automatically a servant swept leaves off the rotten wooden benches though I must have been the only one to have sat in the garden for a long time.

Was Poona with its turbaned ice-cream men on tricycles, door-bell ringing snake-charmers, its Punch and Judy shows starring a magic cow, typically Indian? Had British influence become an integral part of the country? At first encounter I could not judge but that which was purely imitative diminished the quality of the 'real' India for which I looked. By the post office a rosy-cheeked old lady in long black skirts sat in a pony cart with her pomeranian. her Indian servant held a parasol over them as if they were posing for a Victorian photograph. I was on my way to have tea with the Browns, and the old lady stared as I rode by on my bicycle.

Orchids grew on trees in the Brown's garden and they could see the Tower of Silence where, at death, Parsees' bodies were left to be devoured by vultures. 'It's as if they know,' Mrs Brown recounted, 'a cloud of vultures comes circling around before a funeral.' At tea she apologized for the loose-armed chair. 'I was killing a snake with my hockey stick. For some reason it had curled up on that arm.'

It was Mr Brown who disconcerted me by crying, 'If the Lord requires your soul tonight, you'll go to Hell!' I had not been 'saved' he explained after my initial surprise. Why was I travelling, he demanded, 'There is no need to look over hill, over dale for the Truth. Look to the Gospels! There is no greater Truth than the word of God. He sent His only Son to die for us miserable sinners.' I admitted I hadn't found what I was looking for in Poona.

Undeterred, the Browns invited me to a picnic. It would be by a reservoir, 'The same size as the sea of Galilee,' Mrs Brown said. Another English missionary couple and three Indian converts who called each other 'brother' or 'sister', joined us. Mrs Brown reeled off a description of the trees and plants we passed on the way: teak, mango, cork, cotton, the toothbrush tree, the rope plant, the prickly pear cactus, banana, rice and sugar cane. I admired the variety of lush vegetation. Mrs Brown busied herself putting out the lunch while the English girl described her arrival in India. 'I was terrified the first day: all those people lying all over the pavement.'

'How long will you stay?' I asked.

'Oh, it's a job for life.' She had been a secretary in London. 'One day one of my friends asked me if I was a Christian and of course I was terribly insulted. Then she took me to a meeting where I realised what she meant: I hadn't been Saved.'

Her fiancé added that he went, 'Straight from Sunday School, so as to say, to my first job. Hearing the language men used and the things they did to prove they were men of the world . . . .'

I asked, 'What made you become a missionary?'

'When you have something wonderful, you want everyone else to share it!' He hit his fist in his open palm signifying the exclamation point. 'Indians see a white person and make up their minds they will not understand us.'

'So few are even slightly educated,' explained his girlfriend.

He continued, 'We have to live very simply but fortunately we can keep our standards of cleanliness. We never ask for money, it's all voluntary contributions.'

'What happens if none is given?'

'There is always enough,' he replied with a benign smile. 'The Lord provides,' his tiny deep set eyes glistened. 'Do *you* accept Jesus Christ as your personal Saviour?' he began. At that moment a giant lizard saw a beetle and scuttled out from the tree shading us.

The girl said, 'Oh,' in a dejected tone.

'It won't jump,' her fiancé promised, 'just a flick of its tongue . . . .' Snap! Both creatures were gone.

'It *did* jump,' she cried, 'what a huge mouth it had.'

Mrs Brown interrupted, 'We must move our place.' She had noticed ants under the table cloth.

'Oh,' said the girl again. I felt quite sorry for her.

On the way to the picnic the Browns pointed out the Poona zoo. The next day I set out on my bicycle intending to visit it. A confusion of *gharis*, coolies, beggars, women street-cleaners, cycling sheiks and foghorn-tooting buses ended at the town's edge and the countryside began. I stopped and watched women making mud-bricks and stacking them in piles over which a simple kiln would be built. In a funeral the man merely carried the dead child in his arms. I rode by a warren of Untouchables who lived in hovels and their seeming disregard for their own well-being was forlorn.

I heard French voices on the road behind me, '*Si. Si, à*

Damas il y a . . . . ' Two French priests cycled as if they were in the Tour de France. Under the great trees hardly a sunbeam reached the road. Village women carried brass or copper pots on their heads, often a stack of three or four at once, the contrasting metals so highly polished they looked precious, they were. In the distance a man, walking solemnly under his umbrella, descended a grass-covered hill. Boys washed buffalo at a water-hole. I thought I was alone and then looked and saw life everywhere.

I came to a dirt track leading away from the main road and following it to the end, by the river, a temple topped by an ornate dome. A statue of a cow with flower petals scattered over it faced the temple door. 'I wouldn't take off my shoes to go in one of those dens of vice,' Mrs Brown had commented. I parked my bicycle and went down to the bank. After a time I became aware of someone behind me.

A thin Indian with a wispy beard, steel-rimmed spectacles and a loin cloth said at the same moment as I, 'Beautiful,' nodding at the birds, trees and water.

I pointed at the temple, 'May I go there?'

'Why not?' He led the way. We climbed the steps and he asked me to remove my sandals. The low-ceilinged passages ended at a grilled gate and beyond that stood another statue. I realised my guide was the Hindu priest.

'May I give you something?' I offered eight annas which at first he refused, shaking his head until I insisted. We retraced our steps. The austere outer courtyard, the priest guessed was about five hundred years old. He showed me his garden.

'Here is the well. I made it. I heard the Word of God. He told me where there would be water. At night.'

'In a dream?'

'Yes. Come and see where I live.' Overlooking the river was a shelter big enough to cover a reclining man. 'I used to sleep inside the temple but two years ago I came here.' He gazed at the view. A carpet, a heap of fresh flowers, a row of books and a lantern, furnished the room. He picked out a book. 'You can easily learn. One word a day . . . water . . . .'

'Pani,' I answered. He smiled.

'Look,' he opened tins, 'they are all empty, just a little tea left. No sugar . . . .'

'You have nothing to eat?' I was incredulous. 'What will you do?'

'I do not need to ask. God always provides. You gave me eight annas. One anna would have been enough. Do you understand?' His face reflected a smile of secret pleasure. 'I have been here for ten years. I used to be a cloth merchant, then I gave my wealth to my brother and came to this temple. You should be here at night or in the early morning, the sky... I am sorry, I do not speak English well. It is a long time since I practised.'

'Goodbye,' I said going for my bicycle.

'No car? No husband?' the priest asked sounding surprised.

The hostel lunch was the usual curry, whether lamb curry or fish curry, the food was too hot to tell the difference, I couldn't eat either. The fifteen-year-old girl who sat by me had heard regularly from her father who had gone to work in England, until recently. Now the letters had stopped. Like me, she didn't eat and crying, she left the table.

Everyone took an afternoon rest. Even the birds were quiet. A tent of mosquito-net covered each bed. I picked out a book to read by Aldous Huxley finely holed by an insect. The new Bible by my bed was still free of mildew, I noticed and lay thinking how very foreign Poona was despite the fact that everyone spoke my language.

When I was going to return to Bombay, the Browns came to the station to see me off. I gave them money and asked them to leave a sack of sugar for the Hindu priest the next time they went that way on a picnic. Their parting reminder, 'We are all unclean things and all our righteousnesses are filthy rags,' made me heave a sigh of relief as the train began to move.

The Gulf

We were set to sail from Bombay that afternoon and an Iraqi standing next to me at the railings tried to continue a conversation he had begun when he found I was not accompanied by my father, or even a brother, that in fact I was travelling alone. 'I am sorry to say it,' he spoke earnestly, 'in the East women are considered only one degree higher than animals.' The protection he offered me was the last thing I needed now I was on board. I had mentally reserved this week sailing homewards up the Persian Gulf for writing letters.

I had seen just enough of Bombay: it was a good time to leave. Beside the ship, porpoises oozed out of the water like slowly revolving wheels. Lax, skinny Indian passengers trooped by carrying tall glasses, ice rattling, bare feet making not a sound. Porters resembled crabs scampering under loads, scuttling down aisles, they went sideways to avoid me. One was carrying a pair of peacocks in a cage. The owner followed screaming orders. Three boys with rucksacks came aboard in the rush, Germans I guessed. The total of Europeans was now five including me and the woman who shared my cabin. The ship's agent tapped my shoulder, 'Good evening, Miss. Are you comfortable? I'm glad to see you got here safely.' I thanked him. Though the ship had been fully booked for a firm's Indian employees returning to their jobs in Kuwait he had managed to get me a berth. 'All in a day's work. Enjoy the trip, but,' he winked, 'watch out. There is a sheik on board. You had better be careful. There he is now.' I saw a tall man in a brown robe and white *keffyeh* crossing a gang plank. When I turned back to the agent he had gone.

47

Wandering into the silent dining room I found dinner was already being served. The greedy Arab opposite me at table said only one word to the waiter, rapping the duck's breastbone with his knife, 'Pig?' Reassured it was not pork, the Arab took up the meat in his hand and made his enjoyment obvious.

Back in the cabin conversation began slowly. Miss Thomas was an Australian school teacher, on holiday from her job in India. Our second companion, a jolly Indian lady, said, 'Call me Nelly.' We went to bed early. Not a wave rocked the ship.

* * *

The comfortable cabin, the perfect weather, the clean and spacious ship and good food should have made an ideal voyage had not the Arab at table ruined it by the way he gobbled and slobbered. I was surprised he could shake the pepper without making a noise. Always ravenous, he frequently glanced at his watch as if hoping to get through two meals during our one. We ate, eyes lowered, until a great hairy fist flew across for the bread and we were startled into looking up. His teeth would bite through half a roll and then back to the plate would go the remaining piece. I was not alone in recoiling, the others agreed, he was sensational.

'Hello, to where are you going? May I inquire?' The three boys were darkly tanned, their hair sun-bleached.

'You wish my glasses. No?' The middle one offered his sunglasses as I looked up from my deckchair. I shook my head. He went on, 'I am Roulf. This is my friend, Ludvig.' The tallest youth stepped forward and bowed. His face had an unwholesome spirituality, high cheekbones and deep-set orange-brown eyes. Long knobbly fingers pushed back a loop of hair. 'We are from Germany,' the two declared in unison.

'Don't forget me,' the third, the bearded young man interrupted. 'I am Claude. Belgian. *Parlez-vous français, mademoiselle?*' At my affirmative answer Claude sat down easily by me and began talking about his trip around the world. 'I was working in Canada in the centre of winter. How terrible it was, mademoiselle. May I call you Sylvie? *Merci.* I was reading a book about Gauguin. Here is a good idea I think. Six months later I too was in Tahiti, no shoes, nothing.' My attention was captured by a dignified brown-robed figure in the distance. 'I had never seen a kiln in my life but I had to build one for the princess . . . .' Claude's story gathered momentum while the sheik watched his beautiful carpets being unrolled on deck.

* * *

Today's breakfast was half an hour early for shore leave, yesterday the clocks were changed, breakfast was half an hour later. Whatever happened I galloped at the summons of the gong hoping to be finished before 'Pig' arrived. Breakfast was not as painful as lunch or dinner for at the first meal he merely sucked coffee through his teeth, hand on hip.

Miss Thomas and I decided to go ashore and into Karachi by bus. Camels, wearing bracelets of bells above their knees, pulled flat carts or carried cotton bales. They trotted in an untidy way, putting back their tiny ears at the tooting of our bus. 'The authorities tried to alter the left-hand traffic here,' Miss Thomas told me, 'they tried to have everyone change and drive on the right until they realised that they couldn't get the camels to change sides and gave up.' I could not judge if she were being fanciful.

We wrote postcards in the Post Office and walked throught the bazaar. I liked the parrots and fakirs and she the sequin shops, glittering from top to bottom with their samples. We returned to the ship dizzy from incense that smouldered everywhere. 'Karachi bad, yes?' The German boys were already back. Ludvig leaned over the rail and took our photograph, his locks almost obscuring the lens.

Our quarters were dull compared to third or 'deck class', where passengers set up home by hanging curtains, unrolling bedding and lighting paraffin stoves literally on deck. Claude, travelling third class, showed me around. The family camping next to his sleeping bag and motorcycle consisted of a husband, two wives (their faces concealed by leather masks), two children and the grandfather who combed his whiskers for hours with the aid of a little mirror he carried. The husband sitting on cushions, smoked his hubble-bubble pipe while his wives prepared fish caught by the German boys. The family's ducks swam in the scuppers when the decks were washed, their chickens, tied by a leg, roosted on someone's suitcase. Deck passengers had their own souk and bargained for, swapped or bought all they needed. 'It's like the "Arabian Nights" down here. How lucky you are,' I commented naïvely. Claude groaned. 'If I could afford it, I would rather be unlucky and travel first class, thank you.' He pointed to a sheep tethered in a corner, 'For the sheik's banquet tomorrow.'

'How do you know?'

'I have been invited.'

'Why?' I did not mean to sound rude.

'Well, not exactly invited. I invited myself. I begged the sheik if I could take photographs. He said, "OK".'

'I thought you knew the rules, Miss,' the English officer called to me, 'you are not allowed down there with the deck passengers.' He escorted me back. 'For your own good, you understand. That mob down there are a wild lot, they might do anything.'

* * *

Early morning tea began our day. 'Steward!' ordered Miss Thomas, 'Bring tea tomorrow. I don't know what *this* was.'

'I bring tea.' His black face was lost in the dimness, his words floated, devoid of inflection or promise.

At one end of the deck sat the sheik and his company listening to the Koran being broadcast over the loudspeaker. Miss Thomas and I sat at the sunny end. She was prompted to ask, 'Did you hear Billy Graham in Calcutta? No? Oh, I forgot, you didn't get that far. One *can* find true happiness through Christ . . . .'

'*Bonjour* Mees Thomas. *Bonjour* Sylvie.' Claude arrived, cocking his head in the Arab's direction. 'Listening to Mohamet this morning, Mees Thomas?' She changed the subject.

'Just the right heat, there should be flying fish.'

I admitted, 'I'd love to swim.'

Claude laughed, 'Sure, with the sharks!'

'The sea is like jelly bom-boms, sweets I had as a child in

Japan,' Miss Thomas gazed at the water. The ship passed two dhows. Ahead were white sand and palms. The anchor chain rattled, unwinding. An officer signalled the Indian bell-ringer and yelled at the deck hands in Hindi. Claude swung his camera around his neck and clambered down quickly to photograph the dhows. Roulf ran for his fishing line. Miss Thomas sighed, 'I suppose I should write but the printed word is trivial compared to all this . . . .'

The sheik gave his banquet on the top deck. With difficulty the English captain squatted on the carpet and his young officers smirked, waiting, watching to see what they should do next. The sheik, cross-legged and at ease, ate choice pieces placed in his hand. 'Pig' was invited! He gave me looks of self-grandeur when I happened to pass. As usual he was enjoying the food. The feast fizzled out early and a full moon lit an ocean as deserted as the deck.

* * *

Today we were anchored in the little bay of Muscat. Fortresses defended either end of the water-front town and the bright red flags rippled in the wind. Canoes came out, piled with conch shells, silver ones, and cowries. They gathered beneath our bows. Wearing a hat given to him by the captain as a reward for diving under the ship, a negro in one of the canoes cried, 'Next time, black sweater?'

'OK, Tipperary,' called the officers. 'Now let's hear you sing.'

Tipperary began, 'It's a long, long way . . . .'

The chief officer tossed a few oranges overboard. 'Orange! Orange!' Naked children begged and waved from surrounding canoes. Miss Thomas threw them a bar of pink soap and before it could sink children were fighting for it in the water. When blown upon, the conch shells made a hollow moan: a true sea noise. The negroes' eyes rolled upwards as they trumpeted. Passengers caught ropes attached to baskets of shells and pulled them up. Each shell had been tested before it was sent. Waiting, smiling, eyes closed against the sun now, the natives laughed as we blew soundlessly.

The sheik, the only passenger allowed a shore visit, returned in a plunging launch, the ends of his white *keffyehs* held between his teeth so the wind wouldn't carry it away. I noticed he had green eyes. Two goats, bought for the farewell banquet, stood on their hind legs beside him nibbling the rigging. Claude called to us, pointing, 'Look at the new sheeps, tomorrow's dinner.'

'Not *sheep*. Goats,' corrected Miss Thomas.

* * *

Our walks on deck had become an established ritual. 'Why can't they make sensible shoes glamorous?' Miss Thomas remarked. We discussed the morning beverage. 'I think it's 50-50, tea and coffee mixed.'

'No, it's a sort of broth, the top is greasy.' Catching sight of Claude, I shouted, 'Where are we anchored today, is it Arabia?'

'Yes, check it off your list, Arabia – seen.' He and Ludvig paced a lower deck. The weather was oppressive, the jade-green water and colourless sky, unpleasant. For hours the crane swung cargo into the hold, often sacks burst and the porters, glancing hurriedly upwards, scopped what they could into their pockets if no English officer was watching.

'Come. Sheik.' An Arab confronted me and so unexpected was the command that I thought for a second he was speaking in a foreign language. I followed him. The sheik sat in a semi-circle of his company. 'His Excellency invites you to a party tonight,' the interpreter announced and the sheik regarded me without a word.

'Thank you,' I turned and left and went to tell Claude.

It was dark when the carpets and cloths had been unrolled and the steaming silver dishes set out. A single searchlight illumined the robed figures. The sheik led me to my place and I noticed I was the only woman, the only European there. Morsels from the carcasses of the two goats were piled on my plate. Eating rice mixed with sultanas and almonds wasn't easy by hand though I wouldn't have considered using a knife and fork. The food tasted better than any I had had for months. 'Pig' sat next to me chewing at top speed. Hard-boiled eggs were easy to eat, he noticed I had finished one and threw me another. 'Don't be shy!' he urged.

'Good!' was all I could mutter with my mouth full. We ate silently or at least with few words. Walnut ice cream followed, then fruit of which each person chose a piece for his neighbour.

At the end the sheik came and, offering me a piece, said, 'Fresh meat.' Servants then poured water over our hands and dried them. We followed the sheik inside for coffee. A little man with a goatee, his interpreter, brought out ten boxes containing ten identical sets of gold jewellery, like ancient gold, seemingly brighter and softer than ours. Were the necklaces, rings, earrings and bracelets for the sheik's favourites?

'You like?' the interpreter asked. I love gold. I supposed he meant the sheik. The jewellery, the middleman, the protocol, alienated me though I would have liked to talk to him. Did he speak English? According to the Iraqi passenger they had a low opinion of women and might misunderstand my friendliness. With a few grateful words I got up, the Arabs, their faces expressionless, watched me go.

* * *

Soft mountains of sand, oil tanks gleaming, a perpetual orange oil flame in the desert, a pelican drifing beside us, tankers waiting their turn, that was today's port. Arabs in gold-edged *abias* came out by launch to greet our sheik. So numerous were the sons, grandsons, brothers and uncles on the launch that waves splashed over the edge. They stood on the ship's deck emptying salt water out of their shoes until the sheik was ready to depart. After the reunion the whole family filed back down the gang-plank and leaped for the launch with their cloaks flying.

Periodically performing birds, brought up from third class by their owners, entertained us. Charlie the parrot chose cards, jumped through rings and rode in a toy wagon drawn by a pigeon. I held Charlie afterwards. The pathetic bird screeched and flapped in the wind though, of course, his clipped wings wouldn't carry him away. That is how I felt; as though I would never be carried away.

Miss Thomas and Claude had found Nelly, the Indian lady, to be a table tennis champion of such skill that together they could hardly match her. The three of them played all morning and all afternoon. Claude had given me his account of climbing in the Himalayas to read, instead I stared at the sea. The voyage was almost over yet I hadn't the heart for letter writing.

* * *

We disembarked and became complete strangers again. I made for the railway station. The sight from the carriage of grazing sheep in the afternoon sun I could appreciate once we were settled in the train. Travellers had entered Basarah station with a whoop when the gates were opened. Belongings had been merely gathered up in cloths or blankets and these bundles, too wide for doors, had to be stuffed through windows to the discomfort of those already inside. The majority in this compartment were women; travelling we tended to stick together. Their foreheads covered, their faces closely surrounded by black, the old witches, withered and sharp-eyed, flashed their lighters professionally, smoking cigarettes with over-folded hands. Chins tattooed, hands hennaed, ankles bulging with silver bangles beneath their stockings; these were women of the world. Only a young girl nursed a child. Her son pulled at her dress wanting a kiss but it was the station crowd that interested his mother and kept her attention.

* * *

I would have left Baghdad for Damascus if Claude had not seen me in Rachid Street and taken me on his motorbike to the English couple with whom he was staying. 'You speak English awfully well,' observed Christopher, the Englishman, when Claude introduced me. I was English and had met the Belgian on a ship coming up the Gulf, I explained. Christopher invited me to join them on a gazelle hunt. Christopher's wife had just decided not to go, then Claude couldn't because his motorbike needed attention. I helped load the jeep with rifles, blankets, food, water and petrol. A crack shot, formerly of the Palestine police, took Claude's place in the back of the car. Christopher's other guest would be a sheik from a village near Baghdad. As far as I was concerned Arab company gave the expedition authenticity.

By evening we arrived at the sheik's home where he welcomed us in a large hall inside a mud-brick enclosure that also sheltered sheep, goats and horses. Benches lining the wall and covered with carpets later served as our beds. A boy hammered a nail into the wall with the handle of his silver dagger and hung a lantern for us that glowed all night. Warmly covered by sheepskins, I slept well in that nice whitewashed room with beamed ceilings and its smell of milk and hay.

We shared a bowl of scrambled eggs for breakfast. A foal had been born during the night and we admired it before climbing into the jeep. The sheik, cradling a silver-inlaid rifle, sat in the front seat next to me. Dawn came. We rode in silence, our eyes showing above the blankets protecting us from the cold.

After hours we turned off the road onto the hard sand. The windshield was removed, rifles steadied and Christopher driving fast declared, 'This is the moment I love.' The day was overcast, a bitter wind hit our faces. I could not imagine any living creature disturbing the monotony of the vast space.

The morning rewarded us with the sight of no more than a few idiotic camels. Discouraged, we finally stopped for lunch of bread and bully beef. The Palestinian suggested to the sheik he try hitting one of the empty petrol tins dumped some way from where we were sitting. The sheik fired. Silence. Christopher encouraged me, 'You could.' I fired, there was a 'pang'. I had been lucky considering that I had not used a gun since childhood. The sheik became even less responsive. Morale was low.

The first yell came from the Palestinian. I saw a number of horned deer galloping in the distance, their coats blended perfectly with the sand so it was difficult keeping them in sight. Christopher pressed the accelerator to the floor, rifles clicked, clouds of sand billowed behind us. The gazelle separated when we reached them. Swerving, Christopher chose the largest buck. Explosions started. Red stains flecked the animal's coat. The jeep swayed in an effort to follow the dodging creature. A leg was shot away and he fell. I fired, wishing the gazelle would die quickly. We didn't stop or slacken pace, we roared after his mate. When we returned to collect the half-dozen slaughtered animals they might as well have been in a butcher's shop I told myself.

Christopher told me to drive while he searched the horizon with a telescope. Suddenly he saw another herd nearby. I tried to give him the wheel. He cried there wasn't time, 'Drive as fast as the car will go!' The wind blinded me, I went in the direction of the pointing guns. We reached them going on 90 Kph, and they split up. I followed one buck for a minute and the Palestinian killed it with a single shot. I swung around after another, trying not to think about the animal's fear, just about my job of driving.

Afterwards the sheik ceased being cool and congratulated me. Christopher was delighted to find we had killed several more. Some of the gazelle were pregnant. One can't suddenly back out of a situation that one has helped create but it was then, at the sight of the little ones, that I changed sides.

In his telescope Christopher noticed a lorry driven by a couple of youths without guns. They followed the gazelle until the animals' hearts burst with exhaustion. Trailing us in the middle of the shooting, they had stolen one of our dead deer. Fury infected Christopher. The Palestinian was ready to shoot up the boys' tyres, we might have hunted them if I hadn't seen another movement in the distance. Christopher followed my gaze. He turned, driving again, and charged after the next lot at an even madder speed. The gazelle had been in groups of tens and twenties, this next herd must have numbered fifty. The ground became rougher, then abruptly rocky: our tyres were punctured. Although there was very little for them to eat, the deer knew they were safe among the rocks. Because our method of hunting was one degree more humane than that of the boys, Christopher swore vehemently at them for frightening the animals into this refuge.

By dusk, the punctures mended, such frustration overcame the others that they pursued grouse, hare, foxes and even a wolf. We were now far from where we should have been; 'lost' was a word we avoided.

Routine punctures and repairs took place in the glare of

headlamps while the sheik stared into the depth of the engine. Clouds covered the stars. By midnight the terrain had become lumpy with monstrous mounds against which we had to crawl, banging and bumping, our sharp lights emphasizing the nightmare landscape. Spike legs of the dead gazelle stuck out of the back of the jeep. How ugly we looked spattered all over with mud and blood.

We had been hunting south, north was the logical direction to take to hit the east/west road. Christopher drove following the sheik's directions on a south-east course. Looking at the compass I whispered, 'What are you doing?'

'We must not offend Arab convention by disagreeing with our host.'

'*You're* the host.'

'It's easier to drive on his course and then change round when he isn't looking.' A moving light due north eventually revealed the road and half an hour later we had reached it.

'How long now?' I asked. There was no answer: Christopher slumped over the wheel, asleep. I drove. When necessary Christopher woke, automatically patched the shreds of inner tubes, then dropped back to sleep. A final puncture came, one that could no longer be repaired, and uncaring, we fell asleep on the spot.

Clutching two new inner tubes in his arms our smiling sheik woke us the next morning. A Bedouin on camel back had collected them from the sheik's home. As he was going to sit, to the last time, to supervise our work, a passing shepherd boy took off his jacket and put it on the ground for his lord's, my host's, comfort.

Two days earlier the tide of picturesquely dressed people and tooting American cars in Baghdad had amused me. 'What a come-down!' exclaimed Christopher as we crossed the bridge into town. I shared the sentiment. For me the holiday was over. I packed my bag and left for home.

*　*　*

The girls in our London flat were curious to know if I had met any sheiks. After all, sheik-hunting would be their reason to go to the Middle East. I had been away a long time, sent just two cards and to their question, answered only 'Yes.' How could I disillusion them about my holiday? I couldn't explain to them or to myself what it lacked.

To Petra

Even in winter I would have expected to find a lot of tourists in the French coastal town of La Ciotiat; the town had charm. One arm of the port held cafés, private boats and the church. Ships were built there too. A fleet of fishing boats was beached on the sand and nets mended on the promenade. Washing flapped above the narrow streets fresh with sea air. A couple of shops still sold foreign newspapers, their postcard roundabout racks creaked in the wind. In January the front was almost deserted, occasional waves slapped over the sea wall. At the street corner old fishermen gossiped, Buddha-fat dogs squatting by them. 'Why the English come here in this weather . . . .' one was saying in French, his eye on me.

La Ciotiat, not as expensive as Nice or Cannes, was the ideal place for me to wait the three days until I was due to sail from Marseilles. I had always had an *idée fixe* to see a place called Petra and now I was going there.

On Sundays the village seethed, like a net too full of fish, when everyone paraded in his best clothes. On that day I preferred to stay mostly in the garden of my pension. The owner's child talked to me. The fact that he was smaller yet could speak French better than a grown-up pleased him. The little boy's sluggish grey Persian cat crept through the long grass giving looks of startled horror at the explosions of the boy's toy gun or at the dry leaves cartwheeling over the lawn. When called by his mother, the boy was reluctant to go. At last he ran off clicking his heels together. The cat climbed the high garden wall and sat wrapped in its tail with a dignity it lacked at our level.

'What a strong smell of cauliflower!' cried the mother,

romping into the dining room that evening with her usual enthusiasm. Her husband was what is called 'a shadow of a man', with hollow cheeks, stale breath, and lank hair falling over one eye. His three children, *enfants terribles*, took after the mother. Their ruthless enjoyment of life advertised their whereabouts every moment of the day with screams, pistol shots and trumpeting.

Along the road charred stumps marked the trail of summer forest-fires. The pebbly hills were pitted with caves where drawings of prehistoric man had been discovered. I enjoyed exploring the countryside. The one time I asked for directions the man I chose happened to be English. Delighted to speak his own language, he couldn't be stopped. 'Bring your French friends tinned salmon,' he advised, 'or crayfish,' he said on second thought. 'They're teribly expensive in France and your friends or anyone you want to get to know will think the world of you.' He outlined the life of 'them' and 'us' (tourists) for twenty minutes. Frenchmen went out with guns for *Le Sport* pretending to hunt, ready to shoot anything that moved, even leaves falling off trees, according to him. 'I've been here a week already this time and the only money I've spent is on postcards,' he boasted. I could believe it. His repertoire of newsy stories earned his keep. 'They're a bit snooty at first, but awfully *bored*,' he explained. Did customs know him with his heavy rattling suitcases packed with tinned fish? It was his eleventh year in La Ciotiat. 'I never go anywhere else. They get so they're glad to have you back
. . . .'

It was from Marseilles' pinnacle of Notre Dame de la Garde, a hill overlooking the harbour, that I caught the first sight of my Turkish ship with its red crossed anchors insignia. Half-way up I stopped in a café where the waiter serving coffee described the crowds of summer tourists, of how many women 'abandoned' themselves to him. I declined his offer of another coffee saying my ship would sail that afternoon and that I wanted to visit Notre Dame de la Garde. He had never walked that far.

'See the Virgin! See the Virgin!' a man encouraged his wife to climb the last steps to the church. Actually, the gold statue of the Virgin on the building was so big it probably could be seen from a distance of twenty kilometres. 'Oh, Marseilles gets bigger,' the breathless woman said, turning around and looking down on the town instead.

Inside the smell of decaying flowers on the wax effigy of baby Jesus spoiled the air. Those who had survived a trip around the world had made and donated a model of their ship or plane on which they had travelled, to the church. Here they hung, the many different bi-planes, boats, liners and jets. I could well imagine wanting to come to this high place to give thanks.

* * *

The starting of the ship's engines signified the real beginning of this holiday. We slipped out of the narrow berth to the pom-t-pom of the Turkish national anthem. The crew, shouting gutterally to God, leaped about the deck in the half-light, making the ship sea-ready. Waving farewell, passengers were silhouetted against a flaming sunset, and Notre Dame de la Garde behind us, was already floodlit.

Two ships left that evening and the passengers for both waited in the same departure hall. I was going to Beirut, the others would sail to Haifa. 'I am on holiday and I want to do absolutely nothing for the next six weeks,' I told the leader of a group from the Argentine on its way to Israel. He was a medical student who planned to 'work with my hands and ideas to make the desert live again.' For my holiday I had worked hard and spoke almost defensively about my plans to see Petra at all cost. That 'Rose-red city half as old as time,' as Burgon's poem described Petra, sounded romantic.

'You aren't *really* going there, are you?' my landlady had asked.

'Of course,' I pretended to be confident, all one had to do was to keep moving in the right direction. Now the Argentinian had asked me to join them and go to Israel. Speaking French his voice was smooth, in English his words stumbled and his eyes begged to be understood. The sort of man I would marry, I thought like a somnambulist. To his invitation I was too shy to retort, 'You can see I'm not Jewish. I would be such an outsider. How could I go there?'

Ours was an uncomfortable old ship, the iron was rusty, the funnel needed painting but she ploughed determinedly through the rough sea off the coast of Italy. We neared Vesuvius and headed into Naples. I was glad to see the town again and ate well at a favourite restaurant. Afterwards I wandered back; by then our ship was floodlit and how glamorous she looked at night, large and white, moored at the end of the quay.

My steward woke me to announce breakfast was over. I got up, it was just as well to check if he knew the difference between 'over' and 'beginning'. The smooth sea made me wonder at the excellent sailing. I looked out of the porthole. There was Naples. We were tied up again. The officer I found told me, 'The ship is sick. Soon we go. *Ish Allah!*' By God's will!

At breakfast the delicious Turkish marmalade, a transparent thick syrup with peel like bits of red matchsticks floating in it, was worth getting up for at any hour. Christmas decorations of thick paper chains representing garlands of flowers, giant butterflies or fans, still hanging in the dining room, were the prettiest I'd seen. For lunch the mutton came with a fitting sheepy odour, accompanied by rice dyed in three bright colours and topped with greasy almonds. Our evening treat was a cake, a model of the ship with silver tin foil hoists, chocolate portholes, red and pink marzipan flags and mauve rose-buds down the middle. Everyone applauded. Was it the captain's birthday or a special Turkish holiday? I forgot to ask.

A loudspeaker announcement begged us, 'Please put your watches one hour torward, before the day has died.'

'That's nothing,' someone at table commented. 'You were ashore and didn't hear what they broadcast yesterday, 'we have an accident for sale.' There was absolute silence while we thought about what that could mean. I supposed, 'for sale' was forecastle. When I looked over, I'd noticed a big dent in the side of the ship. What could have hit us so hard? Anyhow, now we had sailed and were out of sight of land already.

The ship's doctor was quite solicitous, rubbing my knees, taking my pulse, and asking if I were married. He was tall, thin and wore thick glasses. I felt sick so he fixed me with a hypnotic gaze and said, 'Mademoiselle, the sea is tranquil.' Just then an enormous wave knocked us both off balance.

A hedge of plastic flowers and trees in the salon created a

tropical atmosphere. The captain, everyone's darling, won his afternoon game of *shesh-besh* and gave me a boyish grin. Unfortunately, the barman lacked the captain's easy-going nature. He wore a greying nylon shirt with gold cuff links, lower missing buttons revealed a very hairy stomach. His bar was neither first nor second class, he was adamant, it was 'de luxe'.

In the next cabin a French woman had such a complaining voice that she made even the statement, 'There are many Italians on board,' sound like a calamity. Her Egyptian husband had died, she was going to visit her grown son who had just been divorced, she couldn't buy her special cough lozenges in Naples.... I had not finished giving sympathy for one subject before she left the way open for more. I found it most suitable to look grave and remain silent at her approach.

The crew, who seemed to outnumber the passengers, monopolized the ship in a casual way. My steward had a little head, large stomach and a black high-necked uniform. I got used to his saying, 'Youk. Youk.' a favourite Turkish word meaning 'Nothing', or 'no', or 'not today', or 'I haven't', or 'I don't know', any negative sentiment as far as I could guess.

Passengers got to know each other during the three days the ship took to sail between Italy and Egypt. The dark Syrian, a lawyer, ostentatiously fingered his rosary and made a sly reference to the 'pleasures' of Naples denied to Catholics and Moslems alike. The red-haired Syrian, also a Catholic, spent his days elongated in the salon. The only English couple travelling first-class invited me to tea. The husband had not learned a word of Arabic after working four years as a teacher in Bahrain. 'It's all very well being out there, its an *English* community, he clarified his position. They used to live in suburbia. 'I hated commuting every day, standing in packed trains . . . . Out there we've never had it so good.' His wife wanted to know, 'Do you have Arab toilets down where you are?'

Their little girl added primly, 'I wouldn't use one of those.'

They insisted, 'It's so nice to meet another English person,' which I echoed though I left as soon as I caught sight of the

Syrians on deck and a Swedish girl who was feeding bread to the gulls. A third Syrian, a doctor, drew out a revolver and pretended to shoot the swooping birds. At my approach, he raised his dark glasses as if to aim better.

I said, 'Now I see your character.' His were mouse-like eyes.

He gazed at me, 'I see in your eyes the need of a great, great love.'

The red-haired Syrian started singing, 'Mustapha, Chèrie je t'adore . . . .' The lawyer stopped reading the Bible.

I remarked, 'This song is a bit passée, isn't it?' He readily agreed, nevertheless all three took up its singing with tremendous liveliness. I couldn't help laughing.

They ordered ham sandwiches and a bottle of Scotch to be brought on deck and crossed themselves before eating which I had never seen an Arab do. The red-haired Syrian asked if I liked the English family. I said I did but thought it strange to have learnt no Arabic in four years. 'They have lived like four donkeys,' he made a pun in French. The Syrians' sophistication ended when it came to women, concerning the opposite sex they behave like schoolboys. Though they had a natural passion for words there was little I could talk to them about and if I was quiet, they judged me to be 'melancholy', or, 'thinking too much.'

The French woman left the ship at Alexandria with her son who came to meet her. I went ashore to buy newspapers. A coup had taken place in Lebanon. 'Are you apprehensive?' the Syrians inquired. 'The frontier is closed. You may have to take an aeroplane,' the red-haired Syrian said and confided he was in the intelligence service. Our ship sailed relentlessly towards Beirut. What I supposed to be low cloud turned into land and as we drew near it became a city of skyscrapers backed by snow-capped mountains.

A state of turmoil existed in Lebanon and no one was allowed ashore. After hours only the Swedish girl and I were given permission to land. Machine-guns on the roofs and tanks in the streets impaired my first impression of Beirut. The Swedish girl lived in Syria and offered to share her taxi with me. The sombre trip through the mountains took twice as long as usual, she said, because of numerous police checks. In Arab countries the blonde girl was spoiled and she loved it. Revolutions or coups were nothing new to her. Having seen half a dozen she commented carelessly, 'Governments. They come. They go.' She kindly put me up for the night and as her house in Damascus was near the Amman road it was convenient for my morning's departure.

By lunchtime the following day I had reached Amman. The Jordanian capital's small shops, white houses and crowded streets, covered many hills. I chose a hotel with the advantages of being cheap, central and of having rooms that were not overlooked or noisy, or so I thought. Once inside, the first thing I noticed was a movement on the bed beneath the lumpy eiderdown. I threw back the covers and revealed two sleeping servants clasped in each other's arms. At my enraged summons, the manager apologized, removed the two men and locked the door nervously from outside. A single cry restored my possession of the key. What now worried me was that taps labled, 'hot', 'cold' and 'sprinkler' did not produce a drop of water. I threw open the door to find the manager, happy now to have anticipated my need, holding out a little jug of water. 'I pour for you.' In fact I wanted a shower and to wash some clothes. Told this, he assured me, 'Water at two.' I went out, satisfied, supposing that the pipes were being repaired. I failed to recognize the optimistic phrase used to hide from a guest for as long as possible the awful truth: nothing worked.

Despite a body-search of those entering the well-guarded post office, Amman was calmer than the other two capitals through which I had passed. I visited the museum, and then, at the Roman amphitheatre, a guard asked, 'English girls go to Petra today. You want?' I thanked him. Travelling in a shared taxi was cheaper and easier than alone by a sequence of buses. I found the two girls sitting in the taxi where they had already been for a couple of hours. Of course it would not depart until it was full, I had plenty of time to pack.

We reached Mann at midnight. The hotel we asked for no longer existed according to the driver who hoped to take us all the way to Petra that night. We positively refused to go farther. The hotel we wanted suddenly re-existed.

Kneeling by their beds, the two sisters began their rosaries. 'Holy Jesus,' they murmured in unison. 'Bless us this night. Hail Mary,' they whispered. The big room echoed with their prayers. (They had told me, 'If you are back in Amman on a Monday and want the King's autograph, it is supposed to be possible to get, but telephone the palace first ....') 'Deliver us from evil . . . lead us not into temptation.' They finished praying. The only noise in the room now was from the ticking clock. Paper flowers in a jug and an artificial apple tree were lined up on a table in front of the door which had no lock. 'If anyone tries to enter we will be woken by the crash,' the younger sister cried, laughing happily. A single light bulb gleamed in the whitewashed room. The girls had similar big blue eyes, bony faces, wavy hair, thin hands and cheerful manners. They tried to remember what they had done the day before yesterday in order to complete their diaries.

As taxi drivers quoted an exorbitant fare the next morning we amazed them by starting to walk. News went around town in a flash and one came along at our price. The taxi, already occupied by a South African with a wispy beard and a fat young Armenian had its load completed by the three of us.

Eventually we turned off the King's Highway onto a dirt road leading to Waddi Mussa, the nearest village to Petra. Here the taxi left us. Here Moses struck the rock and the water still flowed. The others drank from the spring along with donkeys while I had a boring preference for my water bottle. Frank, the South African, knew more of Petra's history than the girls who gave the impression they were out on a spree. Their nonchalantly travelling through the Middle East surprised me. As for the Armenian, (what language didn't he know? Where was his luggage? Why no passport or money?) none of us could guess his reason for coming to Petra.

The Waddi Mussa chief of police happened to stride out of his headquarters as we straggled in. To the pretty sisters he cried, 'A good morning to you, sir,' a greeting they acknowledged without a moment's confusion. He referred to us all as, 'hims', showing through, a marked preference for us females and leaving the two boys sitting at the gate while he took us on a tour of his stables. Curiously, he had his horses sorted out. 'A fem-me-*nine* horse!' he would announce as a gentle head came over the top of the stable box. 'Another fem-me-*nine* horse!' he introduced the next and the next, right down the line. When he triumphantly proclaimed, 'The mas-cu-*line* horse!' We dared not look at each other. Needless to say, these thoroughbreds belonged to, and were reserved for, the police. Outside, be-tasselled ponies and noisy donkeys waited, ready for tourist hire.

An English couple, also going to Petra, who had just arrived, hired horses for the last lap of the trip. Frank, and George the Armenian, bargained for a donkey to carry our possessions. We could walk the remaining four kilometres.

Although George could not pay his way he earned it by dextrous haggling. We had a guide, an interpreter, a servant and leader in one. He was both sly and jolly with, at nineteen, a con-man's face of middle age. Despite my instinctive distrust we were soon swearing friendship. 'You, my friend? You *are* my friend,' was George's introductory theme to any conversation. He drew us out and entertained us with his jokes, not a single one of which I can remember.

I bought five kilos of oranges and tied them in a string bag on top of our black donkey's load. Then our caravan set out. Our beast called simply 'Hemar', donkey, was led by a child equally black called A'hemet. Another donkey, scorned by Hemar, carried the English couple's picnic basket. '*Un paysage Mexican*,' remarked the English tourist gazing up at the dull red cliffs. 'He is an English lord,' George informed us. If there was anything George did not know he made it his business to find out. That morning the English couple had driven all the way from Amman in their private car. 'Where did *you* stay in the capital?' they asked me. I told them the name of my hotel in Amman while admitting I couldn't exactly recommend it.

A deep narrow passage, a long crack in the cliffs, called The Suiq, led into Petra making the city easy to defend in ancient times, easy to keep secret until more recent times. No matter how many photographs one has seen, how many descriptions one has read, when one emerges from the gorge into the sun and is confronted by the first ornately carved façade, one is impressed and enthralled.

Earthquakes destroyed town buildings, not the tombs carved out of the rock walls of the site. The Khasneh, that first monumental tomb, from its style and detail can be imagined the richness of the flourishing Nabitead city 1900 years ago.

Wavering layers of pink, brown, cream, in addition to the dominating reds of the rocks fascinated me. 'The Silk Tomb,' noticeable for its ribbons of colour, well deserved its name. Farther up the valley an amphitheatre had been cut from and built into the hill. Traces of shops bordered a paved stretch of Roman road where some columns still stood. At the end, in a clearing under trees, was a camp where the horses were tethered. Once unloaded, Hemar rolled in the sand with groans of pleasure.

I shared my bread and oranges with A'hemet, and a local child who well repaid me by acting as my guide. Alone I might not have found el Deir, 'the monastery', an isolated tomb reached after a steep climb. 'The monastery's' heavy columns, empty niches for statues, cavernous door, and the whole façade surrounded by a giant urn did not strike me as fine, just big. The boy showed me how to climb to the top of el Deir and from there I could see beyond Petra to the west where, shimmering in the heat, the desert was part of Israel.

The child who guided me wore a stocking cap and a man's coat, its cuffs encircled with gold braid, its hem sweeping the ground as he walked. Sniffing, coughing and the swish of the coat followed me as we went back down the hill. Six hundred Bedouin lived in the tombs and caves and all seemed to have colds, TB or cataract. I asked an old man we met, why he stayed in Petra rather than go to a village where life could be easier. He gave a predictable answer, 'Petra is the home of my father, the home of my grandfather.' The boy pointed out a hidden spring, bizarre rock formations, Bedouin shops in caves: things that interested him. Black-robed women squatted by me trying to sell ancient coins they had found, the coins were in good condition, the women haggard.

It was half an hour's walk to the High Place, a wild and lonely spot where an altar bore testimony to ancient sacrifice. A sharp wind brought noises of laughing or screaming. Looking over the cliff edge I saw, on the path below, an Arab woman waving and shrieking. Whether mad or bewailing the dead, she recreated the atmosphere of that horrible place. I kept glancing over my shoulder on the way down as though there were people I couldn't see in the shadows or hidden things behind the boulders.

The sisters' big alluring smiles won them an invitation to sleep at the new hotel in the centre of Petra. They were unaware that their easy acceptance and friendly manner made their Arab host tremble with passionate expectancy. Coolly, the sisters would write their diaries after dinner and then go to bed, locking their door. In the morning they would get up, wash, and say a calm goodbye to whomever paid the bill.

George found a tomb furnished with benches and bright lanterns where we could sleep. The guards to whom the shelter belonged, made us hot soup before going out on night duty. 'Their job is to kill Jews,' George summed it up. Though exhausted I could not sleep and lay staring up at the ceiling where each mark of the mason's tool showed clearly. George snored, he who had done no more than spend the afternoon galloping the English lord's horse. After the lanterns had been dimmed, the guards crept back to their beds. Despite big knives and boastful talk, patrolling on a cold night wasn't the adventure they pretended it to be.

I climbed a hill to see the sun rise and was invited by a Bedouin family into their tomb-house. Metal suitcases made from flattened beer cans held their possessions and only a sewing machine stood in the centre of the room. The woman unrolled a little rug on the floor for me and made tea. I asked the Arab about his four children, three he said, just the three young sons were worth counting. I had a few toffees and balloons for them. His daughter, the eldest, a girl of about eight smiled as I held out my hand to her. Her father, angry she wasn't working, ordered her off to fetch water from the spring. She went with heart-rending sobs. My short visit broke the monotony for her, for all of them, in this prison-like place where they lived.

* * *

If Frank, the South African, made any impression it was slight. His quiet, self-effacing and thoughtful personality was unlike George's. Frank, neither wanting nor needing George's company, did not know how to get rid of him. Since we were all going to the Red Sea port of Aqaba, once more we travelled together by taxi. My objections were ridiculed as

George, lying on the floor at the back, covered by the sisters' coats, came with us through passport control and police checks. The taxi driver seemed to be another friend of his. Again our arrival was late at night. George frightened the sisters by telling them not to swim because the lights attracted sharks. 'Tomorrow you can swim to Eilat,' he joked. The Israeli port faced Aqaba across the bay. No man's land between the two sides was designated by a palm grove.

Frank and George stayed in town, the sisters and I at a water-front hotel. The sisters held court on the 'private' beach the next few days for local Arabs who came to look at girls wearing bathing suits. 'When Arab girls swim they take off *all* their clothes,' the gentlemen informed me. The present display may have been second-best but they did not miss a minute of it.

Outside the hotel gates dozens of new American cars that had just arrived by ship were parked in barbed-wire enclosures. The southern road went to Saudi Arabia. To the north, a kilometre away, was the town of Aqaba. The shops stocked tins of corned beef, boxes of cornflakes, pairs of plaster Alsatians; imported and dusty things. Then I found George sitting at a door of one, who, when he saw me, ordered tea for us though he owned the place. After that, I once more said goodbye to George without much hope it would be for the last time. Actually, I never saw him again. A week later, back in Amman, I encountered Frank on the street looking more pathetic than usual. He and George had been at the same hotel when his money and passport vanished and with them, George. George had talked to me about his home in Jerusalem. Could he have gone there? I was on my way and promised to look out for him.

* * *

I waited at a bus stop on the outskirts of Amman after inquiring at a café and a garage. One person thought he had seen George on a motorcycle. Before the bus came an enormous white car drew up, the window opened and in perfect English the driver asked if I wanted a lift to the outskirts of Jerusalem. Normally I would have ignored such an offer but after one look, to this man I said, 'Thank you.' He opened the door. A machine-gun lay on the seat.

'Never mind', he said, moving it over so I could get in. He drove very fast and very well and we talked about horses which we both loved. When we parted he gave me his card printed in Arabic, saying, 'If I can do anything for you, let me know.'

* * *

I loved Jerusalem at first sight. The hotel the sisters had recommended overlooked no mans' land between Israeli and Jordanian sections of the divided city. Day and night armed soldiers sat on the roof and when I went up to hang out my washing they lent me their binoculars. The Israelis, though, were so close that if I waved, they waved back.

Before the sisters crossed to Israel for the rest of their holiday they promised to signal from the other side but at the appointed hour I forgot to look. The condition on which tourists used the Mandelbaum Gate was that they did not return to Arab countries. As I couldn't bear the thought of having my freedom restricted, I decided to remain in Jordan.

In Jerusalem the gambling games scratched on paving stones by bored Roman soldiers impressed me most after I had visited many holy places of doubtful authenticity. Everywhere I was offered bottles of 'sacred' water and 'holy' earth. Trees, houses, bends in the road were pointed out as spots where such-and-such happened. The whole, not the bits, is important, I wanted to say. According to accounts written by Victorian travellers, they could never have enough mementoes, enough revered shrines. Had the supply at last exceeded the demand?

In the Holy Sepulchre I was distracted by the thought that an old priest reading by candle-light would set his beard on fire. Crusaders had marked their arrival in the Holy City by carving small crosses on the walls. Style varied, it was difficult to see them in the near darkness. A priest, observing my interest, asked if he could show me around. I supposed he wanted to be helpful and followed him. We came to an enclosure in which two could move only with difficulty and here he suddenly began caressing me so passionately that for a second I was paralysed with surprise. Noticing someone's passing he announced loudly, 'The tomb of Jesus Christ.' He raised his hands, finger tips piously touching and whispered, 'I love you.' I quickly extricated myself. 'Stay here,' he implored. 'Come back tomorrow . . . . Have you a friend?' His entreaties reverberated from the shadows as I fled.

I found George's house in the Armenian section of the old city. Its warren of rooms, passages and windows provided escape routes. Everyone knew George though no one had seen him recently. They explained, 'He is often in prison,' as if that were a likely place for me to look. I had done what I could. My week in Jerusalem was over, now the long homeward trip began.

* * *

'If only this hotel had water!' I exclaimed, twirling the taps of the shower next to my room. Since I had been away the Amman hotel manager had had them mended. I was deluged. Once more in a furore of anxiety he was hurt by my laughing and wanting lunch before 'washing clothes,' or 'having bathing' after all the trouble he had gone to.

The police came for me at nine that evening. Why hadn't I registered with them, they wanted to know? As the police examined my passport the card from the stranger with the white car fell out. Picking up the card for me, the police officer glanced at it, then quickly saluted. 'We do not need to trouble you, madame.' He left, bowing. It seemed a member of the royal family had been kind enough to give me a lift to Jerusalem.

For the journey to Damascus I hazarded a visit to the office of *Cleopatra Tours*. 'How old are you? Are you a woman or a girl? Good! Do you come here on your account or for your government? You are welcome. Too much? The train is only three shillings. I wil telephone the wireless station to ask if there is a train this week. Wait! Wait! Excuse me, I have ordered tea for you. But you will go to Damascus, is it not? Goodbye. I WAIT for you . . . .'

The next taxi company I tried, simply asked, 'When will you go?' as if it were a matter for me to decide. The following morning I arrived early for the 7 a.m. taxi. It was 8.30 before I was told, 'You are the lonely passenger.' By nine my bag was removed, a taxi materialized, and a man waiting with a suitcase opened it to place several flat loaves on top of his pyjamas, encouraging signs. I spent my last Jordanian shilling on throat lozenges to prevent coughing. It was a social disgrace to be sick here, possible contagion made one an outcast. At 9.45 I was given the front seat (having waited longest) in the black antiquated Dodge. As soon as everyone was in we were anxious to start, 'Yallah!'

The taxi broke down at Jerash. The wheel would take half an hour to mend. What luck! I rushed off to see the ruins of the Roman city.

The Syrian frontier-guard kept our taxi waiting while he painstakingly searched my passport, checking if former exit and entrance dates corresponded in case at sometime I had slipped over to Israel. He allowed me to get in the taxi again before calling me back by name. My heart pounded. The Syrian guard merely pointed to a car with a Beirut licence plate that had just drawn up at the frontier. Seeing me, the driver of the car asked, 'Beirut? Come if you wish.' I took my bag and with an embarrassed smile got into his car. He handed me a Mars bar. My ex-fellow passengers gaped and looked at each other, scandalized. The driver of the car pointed to a faint line of dust on his collar and grimacing, apologized, 'I am hurried.' Without formalities he was waved through customs and we sped away at 140 kph.

In Damascus he bought cakes for his family. In Lebanon we had lunch at a lovely restaurant almost under a waterfall. The frontiers, the police road-blocks, by that old taxi, they would have taken two days to negotiate; he made the journey in a few hours. Only when someone is nice and respects me as he did, could I relax enough to look back and know how difficult and tiring it is at other times, being a woman alone.

Snow began to fall faster as we reached the mountains that separated the Lebanese valley from the sea. It was dark, large flakes rushed into the lights. We raced at the steep road, wheels spinning, and reached the top of the pass in deep snow. Turning a corner we came across half-a-dozen cars piled up at various angles. I waited for the crash. We hit the nearest, helplessly. Seeing the irate owner get out, he laughed, 'Oh, it's all right. He's a friend, family of the

73

President.' They exchanged good-natured punches. The big cars' ramming each other had done little damage and we helped push them back on the road. He gave a lift to two stranded shepherd boys, saying, 'They will make weight in the back.' They smelled of goat and throughout the trip prayed for Allah's protection. There were ten more serious accidents as well as dozens of abandoned vehicles along the road. He drove brilliantly, passing everyone, being one of the few to get through. I thanked him for the marvellous day when he dropped me at the hostel in Beirut. It wasn't worth thinking where I might have been without him.

No sooner had I sat down by the fire than the two middle-aged Arab-Christian women in charge of the hostel started questioning me about my religion. 'You must pray to the Holy Ghost and believe in Christ . . . . You know *Moslems* wash their feet before praying?' They snickered. I quickly told them about the storm in the mountains. 'Ten accidents!' They raised their hands as if horrified, really they were fascinated and longed for details. I described the kindness of the Moslem driver who had given me a lift. They listened with the clenched-teeth expression of people who dispense facts and can't absorb any. They brought me a cup of tea, saying, '*Christians* can be hospitable also.' Why did they have to *compete*? I was too tired to say another word.

My last act in Beirut was to buy fresh orange juice from a street vendor. Instead of paying double as I had done unknowingly all my holiday, this man gave me the correct change. Being both poor and cheated hurt. I knew then how far I was from becoming as sharp as those with whom I mixed, of becoming a fully-qualified Eastern Traveller.

The ship sailed on a calm afternoon and the officials who saw us off had badges on their caps depicting the cedars of Lebanon. A black and white angora cat floated in the green sea among the millions of squeezed half oranges which formed long ribbons in our wake.

*   *   *

We were loading cotton bales in Alexandria. Souvenir sellers paced up and down the quay with handfuls of slippers and camel-leather bags. They caught passengers' attention, waving their goods defiantly below us, crying, 'Italian money, German money? Madame, only ten shilings!' Horse-carts rattled over the cobbles. It was a long port and ships from many countries were being loaded there. Minarets rose above the skyline of warehouses and modern block hotels. The sand and sea were pale grey and the sky, Wedgewood blue, filled with low clouds. On the haunting cold breeze I could smell the cargo of snails we were taking to Marseilles.

We sailed out of Alexandria to the music of tea-time violins. A flock of fat Egyptian women clustered around a window for a last look at home. Their scent was stupifying. They told each other, in French, what precautions they had taken against sea-sickness. Individual buildings no longer stood out. The sea was rough and dark. 'How's the blonde?' asked a new passenger.

'How's the cowboy?' I responded. He smiled and raising his large-brimmed hat, revealed a giant scar.

'German bayonet,' he explained.

'Is the hat to hide it?'

'Yes, otherwise people would think I was a gangster.' He was a Jew going to Venezuela, 'For a new life.'

From where I sat on the top deck the ship seemed to be moving in the heavy swells with tremendous lassitude. A steward, crawling on hands and knees pounced, but missed catching the bird that was taking a rest. Wrapped in my Bedouin blanket, Jacqueline, a Jewish child of thirteen sat by me, staring at the sea. On the other side sat an Armenian. He held the book he was reading with both hands so the pages wouldn't flap. We three were inseparable and because they didn't speak English they adopted my French pronunciation which made us laugh. That was the way we lived for a week between worlds.

* * *

Spring had arrived in the north of France, chickens scratched in the wide ploughed fields, the willows were tinged with green.

* * *

'Have your tickets ready, please.' Smoke drifted out of thousands of little English chimneys. The sun was weak, the grass looked dead. Suddenly, I was afraid I was going to find another strange country ahead of me instead of home.

The Detour

'Persia. Oh my goodness,' cried the young Englishman on the Orient Express.

I had answered, 'Teheran', casually when this fellow traveller asked where I was going.

Enthusiastic and curious about my trip ahead, he did not inspire reciprocal interest. He was the only other passenger in the compartment and on his way to join a German choir for Christmas. The Englishman read *The Times* and drank his aunt's peach wine before changing into a nightshirt and going to bed. I thought of the French soldiers on the train during my last holiday who had drunk *vin ordinaire*, read comics, and just slid their caps forward over their eyes as they lay down. They had looked away when I changed my stockings, a consideration that made me remember them. The Englishman, on the other hand, by trilling and testing his voice just before we reached the station, the next morning, woke me at 5 a.m.

During a brief stop in Milan the excellent Italian coffee restored my spirits. Local people got on the train: housewives and businessmen, not the sort I had expected to use a long-distance express. One woman shared her cooked chicken and even those who had already eaten lunch accepted a piece. When they left I felt the party was over. By evening the train had rolled into Venice, and out again. For kilometres I saw nothing through the white fog wafting from the water.

The second morning frost-covered windows partially revealed the flat landscape of Yugoslavia. Two droskies waited at the station, the fur-hatted drivers paced wearily up and down to keep warm and their nags, tattered sacks across sharp backs, swung their heads after them, ears flattened in irritation. The droskies were filled with straw and in one several passengers sat nestled like huge wrapped-up eggs. The second horse started to run when our train whistled and its driver, like a mechanical toy unwinding too suddenly, galloped after it. Steam rose, hiding the few dumpy cottages, the geese and piles of freshly chopped wood. The train's whistle had a chilling screech; we were moving again.

When a Turkish family came into the compartment I knew I was on the wrong train or at least in the wrong carriage. The women wore baggy flannel trousers and brightly printed scarves. They had low foreheads, large flishy mouths and wet-raisin eyes. Whenever they heard a baby crying elsewhere on the train they turned their heads towards the noise attentively, as mother-animals would.

The restaurant car provided peace, a cup of tea and a chance to stretch my legs. By now I had the sensation minutes might be hours, or of hours merging into minutes. The waiter's unshaven face, the creased white table cloth or a glimpse of what was Greece, of a goat standing on the steps of a house, all touched my tired eyes like sharp images. My mind was blank.

Passengers had multiplied and lay sprawled so thickly that I re-entered the compartment with difficulty. The windows were steamed over from the inside and the worn, perspiring faces might have been suffering from seasickness. I opened the window, everyone revived. The children reached out hungrily when I passes round a new packet of figs: three came back. The peasants' lunch and supper consisted of black bread and water. Exhausted, the old grandmother sucked a lump of sugar, took it out half-finished and gave it to one of the babies. She told the older child on her lap to stand and he stood, wobbling, propped by people's knees, trying to steady himself, he caught his finger in the sliding door. Papa commanded him harshly not to make a sound so he wept silently, his shaved head bowed, a red bandana around his neck. The adults watched me reading and writing. None of them could do either. There was no way of telling them that such an ability seemed as amazing to me.

The blinds were drawn tight and dust remained thickly unbreathable from the sweeper who had just passed. Giving its screaming whistle the train shot through the night, no longer could I guess in what direction. Dinner, they said, was at eight-thirty. On the dot, I went to the dining-car, opened the door to see swirling smoke and track. In my eagerness I had almost stepped into space. Desperately I hunted for the ticket-collector, who, when found, confirmed that mine was a local carriage due to be disconnected at the next station. He installed me in the correct one indicated by dim, shaded lights and pom-pom tassled upholstery. An elderly lady sat in one corner, a Persian student in the other. At least I would arrive on the Orient Express with people like myself who could take comfort and plenty for granted. In Italy couchettes had mysteriously disappeared but in this compartment there was room to sleep. I slept, dreaming of a Turkish woman who cut a single orange into slivers, one morsel for each child to mouth for hours and hours . . . .

I awoke to see the Turkish symbol of a crescent moon and star engraved on each window. I asked the Persian if there were still earthquakes in his country. He replied, 'Finished.' I asked if it were Christmas. After much backward fingering in a Persian diary he said, 'Yes,' then 'Istanbul. 12 or 2. Maybe.' Four and a half days ago I had left London.

In Istanbul my hotel was behind the Blue Mosque; roads were rough and unpaved, upper balconies of the wooden houses jutted out over the streets, white horses, their tails tied in knots, trotted fast up or down the hill, pulling their rattling wagons. Chickens and children are expected but the number of cats was of plague proportions. A bread shop painted blue adjoined my hotel, piles of kindling for the ovens and a willow tree leaned against the buildings. Loaves were delivered, to the sounds of passionate he-hawing, in big baskets strapped to either side of a donkey. Ruins were entwined with ivy, gaps in the cobbles filled with grass; in this port of Istanbul town and country touched. My eyes kept returning to the gold dome of the mosque shining in the blue sky. I felt impelled to go there. Goats grazed and lilac grew inside the mosque's courtyard. I walked up the steps and, taking off my shoes, pushed aside the leather curtain. Sunlight streamed over the rosy carpets which covered the vast interior. Chandeliers on chains so long that they hung just above my head were suspended from the high dome.

79

Blue-flowered mosaics decorated the arches, encircling the columns were gilded bands of quotations from the Koran. Fluttering pigeons and the uncoordinated ticking of two grandfather clocks, their brass pendulums catching the sun, made the only sounds. A few men kneeling and prostrating themselves far from me, prayed silently. Eventually it was my freezing bare feet that forced me to leave.

I ate at Galata bridge where fishermen tied up, cooked and served their catch in their boats. The sea churned with the activity of large ferries and swarming small craft, a flapping red Turkish flag on every boat. Countless minarets rose above the skyline. Gulls by the hundreds floated on the choppy sea. Over-crowded, lethargic Eastern towns are often described as 'teeming', an adjective that suited Istanbul. The moody sea and western sky refreshed me, here was the best of both worlds.

'Blinding' described displays in the gold bazaar. Stocked with gold and pearls each small window was flood-lit, passages between the shops, dark. I went from one to another admiring little mountains of bracelets, each 'set' fastened together with a safety pin. Pendants came in the form of Madonnas, Stars of David, *La Main de Fatima,* horses' heads and Eiffel Towers, providing something for everyone. If I were rich I would share the Eastern woman's preference for wearing her wealth rather than depositing it in a bank. The silver shops came next, then the antiques, furniture, cloth, spices and after walking hours I'd seen a fraction of the bazaar.

On the way back every afternoon I stopped by the Blue Mosque. Its lamps cast a very pale yellow light after sunset. The chestnut-seller, bent over his glowing charcoal brazier at the steps, would press a hot nut into my hand; a gesture as simple as this made me feel at home.

I awoke to hear foghorns on the Bosphorus and the wailing call to prayer. Then a mouse ran over my pillow. It was useless to scream. The only other room with a view of the sea in this working Turks' boarding house was occupied by two girl missionaries, self-appointed, 'Not even professional,' they told me.

'But if you have converted one person, you're professional.'

'Oh, good,' said the spotty girl after they had thought about it. 'The Turks have no hope of Eternity, nothing to live for,' she elucidated. 'We can, at least, give them that.' I was curious.

'Will they listen to you?'

'Oh, we're careful to make friends with them first,' she confided, 'we have to try to make them think we are *interested.*' The hotel-owner tolerated the girls good-humouredly as women who would be all right once they were married off.

I caught a bad cold. The proprietor, offering to have a meal sent up, promised, 'What you want, we will get.' Always in the East there hovers the illusion of miracles. I would have liked a mushroom omelette, camembert, crusty rolls and a chocolate-nut sundae. I knew I would get nothing like that for a couple of months. After an hour the owner brought me yoghurt, a loaf of bread, half a dozen hard-boiled eggs and some oranges, exactly the things I had learned to ask for in Turkish. Because I couldn't say 'hot meal', everything came cold, in a paper bag. The moment I was better I asked the hotel-owner to recommend a good cheap restaurant. He did. It was fantastic. I ordered for two. The restaurant owner was delighted, he served me enough for four.

Having solved the problem of where to eat, I mentioned the mouse problem to the missionaries. The next time they came into my room they saw the mouse run under a loose piece of linoleum. With unexpected speed the husky girl flattened the lino with her foot and we heard the cry of squashed mouse. My dislike for them was such I could hardly thank them. 'Oh, don't worry,' they consoled me, 'it's far too cold in here, it won't start smelling for ages.'

Along the path to Topaqi, the Palace of the Sultans, a row of cannon lay in the grass, an old woman conducted her sheep home, sailors were eating berries and children chasing iron hoops. From there I had a shifting view of a grey and blue turbulent sky and a sea that always seemed to be at high tide.

Topaqi's rooms served as a museum for its collection of ceramics, arms, costumes, painting and jewels. The ermine cloaks patterned with crescent moons of fur, high crimson velvet boots, dressing gowns embroidered with climbing

81

roses for very fat men were so vulgar, so splendid, they were suitable only for sultans. Huge emeralds and rubies made up the opposing sides of a chess set. Bed-spreads encrusted with pearls, desks inlaid with amber, cages or candelabra made from porcelain or glass, as well as from solid gold; these precious things lost importance when seen in such quantity. I would have given the rooms full of Sèvres for the Isnik plate on which was painted a giraffe tied between two trees.

Stained glass windows of the council room overlooked a lily pond. The low gold-cloth covered couches, charcoal braziers, peacock fans and cushions lay as they were left I would have liked to believe. Red and gold curtains had been pulled back to hide their shredded tears of age. To get from room to room I crossed an avenue of cypress on a cobbled court. A new moon turned yellow. All the guards had colds, I could hear it in their voices. They directed me so I would be sure to see everything. The arms museum bristled with hatchets, coats of mail, bud-shaped helmets, rifles the length of spears, cross-bows covered with silver flowers. To the attentive guards I commented, 'Beautiful,' or, 'Very beautiful,' in their language.

'From where you learn Turkish?' They were pleased even though thirty words were all I knew. The harem had an atmosphere of its own: small, round, domed sky-lights lit the narrow passages instead of windows, baths were of marble, beds, the width of rooms. This palace of Topaqi revealed a Middle East I was born too late to know. I didn't mind, the present captivated me.

This year Teheran was my objective. It would be a simple trip via Baghdad as the Express left Istanbul punctually three times a week. I asked a friend in the Iraqi capital to meet me and reserve a hotel room for a few days. Fate interceded within a few hours. We had got no farther than the Taurus mountains when a blizzard brought our train to a standstill, fortunately. We learnt later the railway bridge ahead had collapsed. The detour would add twenty hours to the trip, announced the official who came down the corridor, knocking on all doors. Our faces fell, we had hoped he was someone selling sandwiches. I thought of my well-travelled friend in Baghdad who would surely expect trains to be late? Six weeks late as it happened. He had given me up for dead by then, he said.

On the Baghdad Express an Arab named Ali occupied the opposite seat. Breathing heavily, he made himself at home by spreading out his blankets. His movements, thinness and hairy hands reminded me of a spider. Frequently his umbrella crashed off the luggage rack. He kept combing his hair and looking out as though expecting an important visitor. I found myself doing the same. Then his umbrella would hurtle through the air and again his apologies would follow my cries. After an Istanbul holiday, Ali was returning to the university in Baghdad. The more facts he forced on me, the stronger became my aversion but his determination, 'to make a party', gave me no choice except to listen. Ali had a passion for writing everything down. If I misunderstood his English he would mark his mistake in a little book. Finally, when I closed my eyes pretending to sleep he busied himself with another pastime, though before doing so he hissed in a voice loud enough to wake me in case I had already dozed off, 'I'm writing my *drama.*'

The train's stopping woke me. One had to be quick signalling the children who sold bread and hard-boiled eggs on the station platform. Ali, declaring that the town was famous for carved pipes, got out to buy one. 'Isn't it dangerous to leave the train?' I suggested. He was not back by the time the train moved again and I wondered whether to drop his bag and umbrella out of the window. Ali, at that moment, reappeared, a huge carved pipe clamped between his teeth. My relief was followed instantly by a more rational disappointment.

A mother with two young children who had just got on started preparing a meal on a paraffin stove. Ali watched. He was unable to contain himself. He offered to supervise the stove and took over. Suddenly a whoosh of flame filled the place. We crowded at the door which Ali had locked. There were screams, the woman with the baby threw herself over the child. No harm was done, however.

Snow turned into rain making a dark and soggy landscape. Ali sang aloud the prayers from his Koran until interrupted by a man selling scent. I thought it smelt like rotten vegetables. 'One lira,' Ali held up one finger, intending only to insult the perfume dealer, instead he was sold a tiny bottle of the putrid stuff, and dabbed with some for good measure. Periodically I went to search for another corner seat. There wasn't one on the whole train.

In due course two Syrian sheiks replaced the woman and babies. The men regarded me whenever they turned the pages of their newspapers. Their faces were the kind that looked as if, for generations in their families, nothing had mattered except sensuality. With a grand manner, in gold-edged cloaks, they reclined across the seats as if very comfortable, as Ali and I were squashed in the corners, they probably were. Soon Ali got them to talk. Words such as 'Vietnam', 'Gamal Nasser' and 'Palestine', cropped up in their conversation. Ali translated from Arabic to English the questions the Syrians wanted to ask me. 'What do people in Britain love, Arab or Jew?'

I replied, 'Truly, the people in England live on an island and think like that: they love neither Arab nor Jew, they love themselves.'

'And will you tell them the Truth?'

'Yes,' I said. 'We all look for the truth but God must show it to us.' My saying little and talking a lot earned their comment, 'You speak well.' I heard Ali's 'drama' was in being a Palestinian.

The Syrians muttered, 'If there were a Jew here I would kill him,' (a cut-throat gesture). Would my sympathy for Jews merit death or merely expulsion, I wondered? I looked into their eyes, wishing I could really communicate.

'If a Jew were sitting here,' Ali explained, 'I would not kill him. He has taken my garden. I would take *his* garden.'

At the next station the Syrians threw their hard bread at a stray dog, calling, 'Here Johnson, here Johnson,' in a pathetic attempt to insult the American president. Although I tried to introduce other subjects, the atmosphere of hate persisted.

At the frontier, in the middle of the night, the Syrian guards took me off the train. My passport was not in order. Their consulate in London had given me the wrong sort of visa, incorrectly stamped. It was final. The guards stood around a fire in their full-length sheepskin coats. The snow fell. The Baghdad Express departed with its lights and warmth, leaving me in darkness except for the flames. I crept into an empty carriage beside the main track to sleep. It seemed like the end of my holiday, the end of the world, in my mood.

Far from it. Hours later the carriage I was in began to move. It had become the Mersine Mail train. Where was Mersine? No one was going there except the driver, the postman and me.

As always I was found, this time by a little girl on the Mersine platform who asked if I spoke English. She studied English at school and invited me to her home. I went, hoping to discover where I was but her parents spoke only Turkish. They made signs that I must stay with them for the night and I did. Sleeping on the mail train I had been bitten across my face by bugs and such ghastly red weals made me 'unclean'. In this condition, hospitality was unexpected.

Gradually calm came back to me. The house contained one large room and two small rooms for a family of fourteen. Lack of privacy, had I stayed longer, would have become intolerable, as it was, for the two weeks I remained with them I was happy. They gained a certain prestige in harbouring a foreign visitor, and by contributing a fish or some fruit every day I tried not to be a financial burden. They were not poor, just generous and impoverished by the number with whom they shared everything. Breakfast and lunch (until I added to it) consisted of bread, a little cheese and sweet tea.

Irfan hurled the top I bought him onto the floor, he couldn't make it spin, neither could I. The old grandmother, fat and wise, prayed on her little yellow mat. Sitting cross-legged on a bench that ran the length of one wall, the father read a newspaper after meals. Above him, on the whitewashed wall, hung a dried rabbit skin and a bunch of oranges with leaves. The pregnant aunt removed the swan-shaped pottery jugs that held our drinking water, then vigorously scrubbed the table. The floor was brushed and bench-rugs straightened by the children. The mother lay the baby between her legs on the carpet and rocked him by rocking her body. When he slept she threw her cardigan over his face and with the others began clapping rhythmically and singing Turkish songs. They smiled, waiting for me to smile. The grandmother, having finshed her prayers, recited with almost breathless excitement the alphabet in English, all she remembered though American-born. As a young girl she became a Moslem and returned to Turkey, her family's country. Learning that I was not a Christian, she offered to make me a Moslem. I believed in one God, that was all. I tried to tell her and I think she understood.

A new jetty was being built on one side of town. In the old section of the market, around the palm and pine-tree filled square, horse-cabs waited, and baggy-trousered women readjusted their burdens or swaddled babies. At the café adjoining the mosque, men sat on fine days under trellises of yellowing vine leaves. Roses and poinsettias bloomed in the public gardens. Fresh heaps of cabbages, radishes and oranges were sold in the market. I liked going for walks. In the house one had no self, even the children's homework was considered anti-social. I too, was interrupted. Although they could not talk to me they thought I shouldn't have such lonely occupations as reading or writing. Repeatedly they would take the book (how I wanted to get on with Proust) out of my hands. They longed to get me back into their orbit. The children were happy without toys. They loved their mother's songs and gathered around her when she squatted on the floor, kneading dough by the stove. We drew pictures of animals, exchanging Turkish names for English ones. The women couldn't resist asking me to send them patterns of the latest fashions from London though their religion forbade bare arms or head, or an immodest hem or neckline.

In the afternoon other families invited me to their homes for lemonade and Turkish delight and to look at family photographs. The responsibility of being the first English person to whom most of them had talked inhibited me; they took my nationality very seriously and my presence as that of an ambassador. The subject of Cyprus was a nightmare, no one seemed interested in talking about the weather.

A wild, windy morning followed a night of torrential downpour. They brought in a frightened bird and put it to dry under the stove. Seeing branches being blown off the eucalyptus trees, the mother shrieked for the safety of her two children who had just left for school. The grandmother prayed philosophically; she had lived through many storms and thought only of calming the others. The baby with a puffy, Blake-like face, sat frowning on his pot. I followed the children and watched them dodging spray as they ran down the beach. Rolls of sand-coloured waves rushed up with

Atlantic ferocity, palms had their plumage skinned back, fishing boats waited at anchor, their black crescent shapes taking turns dipping out of sight behind the breakers. I saw the pink and green curtains of the café flutter, even behind closed windows, and the faces looking out seemed to press forward with interest.

In the evening the women collected to watch me undress. They could not believe I would change my clothes and take a cold (no hot) shower every day. The schoolgirl thought such ways would 'kill' her. The grandmother inspected my figure and gave my breast an approving slap. Her verdict was transmitted by the girl, 'Stay with us and my grandmother will marry you to a very beautiful man – a doctor!'

'I am going to Persia,' I said. The Turkish family could not believe a distant, strange place would have any attractions after the town of Mersine. At last, with many goodbyes, and the feeling my destination was indeed far, I arrived at the station. Until the train started even I had doubts about my leaving. Then we picked up speed, the train sounded its challenging toot to whatever might be in its way and all my excitement to see Persia returned. I looked for an ideal society, one in which I would enjoy feeling at home. Perhaps such a thing existed in Persia, perhaps it did not exist at all, perhaps it existed in Mersine for those who knew no other way of life.

These Express trains running from one side of Turkey to the other were good, and the weather had improved. In a few days I had reached Erezurem, near the Eastern frontier. 'Russe! Russe!' people cried, flinging out their arms, their palms upward to express the limbo to which I and the train would travel if I did not get off quickly.

A horse cab, its black hood hiding me, a bunch of narcissi pinned inside smelling intoxicatingly sweet, transported me from station to hotel. Wrapped in sheepskins, the driver whipping his galloping horse and those of any other cab within reach, brought us careering through the snow, past minarets and misty bare trees, along twisting streets, to a hotel called, I think, the Eden Palace.

In the hall of the hotel a smoking wood fire half blinded me. How would I find the bathroom? Was there a bathroom? How could I extinguish the formidable oil-lamp they had

87

given me for my room? Anyhow the bed was soft and clean. I could not understand what people shouted outside the door, and when they knocked, I shouted back, 'Yarin! Yarin!' Tomorrow!

The next morning I found those I suspected as being villains, supposed I was mad. A woman travelling alone must accept the protection that men not only offered but which they considered their duty to give. Why had I locked myself in my room? Why had I clutched my passport? They would send it away for an exit-stamp. What was this talk of buses? There was one a week and it had gone two days ago. My transportation had been arranged with another traveller, in his private car. I gave up my passport, got into the motor car and thanked them.

Before night we had had an accident, not to our car, to the car following us. The man, whose passenger I was, said his friend, a bad driver, had become a much worse one since killing a pedestrian. I looked at the other car's torn fender and bent wheel and at the military lorry with which it had collided, plunged nose-deep in a snow drift and felt relieved that the damage was no worse. Accompanying his friend's damaged vehicle, we drove tortuously slowly the five kilometres back to the nearest village. A trip alone in winter could have been dangerous so both cars stayed close together.

I loved the expanse of sun and snow here more than anywhere else. (Lapland had seemed a bleakly clean land, lacking the mellow maturity of the Middle East and didn't appeal to me.) The only sleigh we passed was driven by a man in a black sheepskin coat. He had a woman passenger cocooned in white woollen shawls and their horse wore a necklace of blue beads for luck.

At the village, in a shed, both drivers worked on repairs with borrowed tools. The second driver's passenger, also Persian, stayed with me, chewing dried sunflower seeds. My gaze was irresistibly drawn to his splendid gold teeth. An articulate woman's voice on the car's radio prompted the information, 'Moscow,' from the gold-smile Persian. On the hour he turned to the BBC. The sound of Big Ben striking summed up the whole world I had left behind.

Coming out of the shack where they had been working for

hours, the drivers waved bloody hands, shook their heads and made the signal of sleeping here tonight. No sooner had we taken our blankets and locked the cars than an awful siren blew. All the village lights went out. We stumbled over icy rutted streets towards the only hotel. The boy who slept against the door as a guard finally woke at our shouts and showed us four beds in the corridor. Into them we fell, asleep, fully dressed.

At five the drivers started work again and though it was dark and still snowing, the Persian and I sat downstairs waiting for tea. Grudgingly the boy remade the fire, took a bucket of water, sloshed some on his face, some on the floor, and began sweeping. The Persian broke his bread in half and gave a piece to me. An hour later the cars were ready. We set out in a joyous mood; they were going home. When daylight came sky and ground merged into a blanket of white, they followed a road invisible to me. We saw no one until noon, where at the highest point of the pass a snow-plough started work.

A single building beside the road indicated the Persian frontier. We raced towards it. As we reached it a crowd of little men burst out, crying and waving bouquets, they rushed at the car. For a moment I thought we were being attacked, then I realized these relatives of the drivers had, because of our accident, been waiting at the frontier two days to welcome them. On occasions such as these each brother, each cousin brought a friend, each sister sent a fiancé. The drivers of the two cars had been abroad five years, the number who greeted them proved how much the boys had been missed. Detained by customs officials, the drivers opened the gift boxes of nuts and sweets and handed them back to their hungry family who ravenously helped themselves. The relatives sat in the waiting-room, two to a chair, talking in whispers, giggling behind their hands and flicking imaginary dust off their American-style clothes. My layers of sweaters and blanket-like full skirt made me too large to share a chair with anyone. As happened here, my first impression frequently remains valid. I found in Persians I met then and later, the same delicacy, sensibility and nervous energy. No matter how much I wanted, throughout my Persian visit, to fraternize, I lacked their qualities and felt conscious that I remained as I had been, a large awkward lump, sitting alone on my chair.

Formalities over, we drove to the nearest restaurant, one of those whitewashed rooms with neon lighting and a long table down the middle. The men played an assortment of instruments, beat the table, sang, danced and ate. This evening of intense celebration was my introduction to Iran.

We had been up for twenty-four hours by the time we reached their village. My driver pointed out the thin strip of gold sequins in the black distance which was his first sight of home. Our convoy of welcoming Buicks and Cadillacs had increased ten-fold, lights swarmed after us as we led at a speed best described as careless, considering the unmarked dirt road, the rocks and chasms. At dawn we entered the grey streets. The high mud-brick walls, the rows of bare poplars and silver birch, the blue doors of houses and women wrapped and hidden in a single covering had, in common, an aesthetic quality.

From the luggage compartments of the new American cars live sheep emerged that were walked away by the hind legs to the kitchens. Enormous, prolonged, welcoming feasts got under way in the house of the drivers' father. Though it wasn't the gracious thing to do, I asked if I might retire. A room papered with a bold green geometrical pattern that jarred on my tired senses was ready for me. A servant brought breakfast of mint tea, honey-comb, cream cheese, and a bundle of light brown Iranian bread, as thin as paper. The driver, the eldest son of the household, returned to give orders to girls seated around me whom I thought were his sisters. They jumped up either to get me more tea, or to offer pistachio nuts from silver boxes. He told me they *were* his sisters, that *I* was a sister. With a limited vocabulary he expressed what he meant well enough.

A man responsible for a woman honoured that obligation to the end. Time and again, a bus-driver who had looked after me, would pass me on to a policeman who would hand me over to a hotel-owner, and then *he* was responsible for my well-being. The owner of a little Baghdad café where I ate alone at mid-day every day threatened (quite rightly) to kill a man who sat at my table and started talking. I had to slip quickly out the back door before anything worse happened. I was glad to inspire protectiveness and tried to act in a worthy way. Although longing to stare about, I travelled with demurely lowered eyes as was expected. Probably this attitude to women, this respect for even a European woman, has by now changed or vanished but so too has my desire to travel.

My host showed me to another room with a variation of the green geometrically-patterned paper. The open bed revealed sheets of brown satin, quilts of rose plush and a velvet pillow, decorated with a scene of hounds, horses and stags. Glistening atomizers stood on the lace table cloth, above, Marilyn Monroe smiled reassuringly from a calendar. I pulled the quilts over my head and slept. I knew the room my host had given me was his.

Sun was already coming through the gauze curtains and spliced bamboo blinds when I awoke. Big potted lilies lined the window sill. From the window I could just see the high wall of our compound and a few bare trees above it. The servant lit my oil stove, washed my clothes and brought me tea. Her name was Tamar, she had a Mongolian face and wore trousers under a skirt, thick woollen socks and for out of doors, slippers with the backs turned down. In this magnificently carpeted house no one wore shoes.

The first day I intended to leave and on the second and on the third. One of the sisters had a French-speaking friend who translated for me. She said, 'Don't go outside please, everyone will look at you.'

'But the bus!'

'The bus has departed.' If we did leave the house it was in a motor car. I in the middle, the girls on either side, swathed in chadurs covering all except their eyes. In this way we went to tea with an elegant lady whose cups of solid silver were awfully hot. Whenever I contributed a word, taught by the sisters, to the conversation they clapped their hands. I had nothing else to do yet became absolutely exhausted by smiling continuously.

Always trying to 'entertain' me, they took me to a Hollywood film. The national anthem played while a picture of the Shah was projected on the vistavision screen. We came out to a full moon and a sky filled with luminous El Greco clouds. Fireworks exploded, flags hung out of every shop, it was a public holiday celebrating the day Muhamet was called by God to become a prophet. Was there more night-life here than in Arab villages, or was the activity due to the festival? A difficult question, though nothing was impossible to ask. I am shy and at home would not dream of performing the absurd mime required to give or ask for information, as I did in countries far from my own.

The house in which I stayed had a pool in the garden where the women washed their chadurs. Their loose slippers flapped as they walked quickly back and forth, their cotton skirts were rolled up, revealing other skirts and trousers. They worked thoroughly in the splashing cold water, hanging up the navy blue chadurs (only semi-circles of cotton), a plastic table cloth, and the men's shirts. A Persian cat sat in the shadows beneath the line and two eagles ate scraps with one claw while perched on the edge of the roof. The servant, on the way out, almost had her chadur blown away, so, giggling, she tied the corners behind her head in a bow and waving her now free hands, ran off to answer the pounding at the door. A man had come with a tree and began to dig a hole in the garden. Tea was brought to me, then almonds, then a cake, then because a sister was eating one, a boiled potato. Everything was shared. She ate with me in the garden, squatting, the chadur completely over her head, eating unseen in the presence of the digging man. The brass gate-knocker in the shape of a hand crashed again. Tamar arranged her feet into slippers and rushed off, to find, this time, a woman selling bolts of cloth.

We kneeled on the predominately red carpets in front of a silver samovar. The only other things in the room were a giant silver alarm clock and a cat that trod our knees with puffy feet. Touching or looking at the bolts of material that had been tossed in the corner was avoided, the women busied themselves with tea, putting a lump of sugar in their mouths and drinking through it. At the appearance of the gardener to report he had planted the tree, the women covered themselves, it seemed to me, in panic haste. Having left her chadur out of reach, the grandmother dodged behind the curtains where she remained giving orders until the door had closed and the man gone.

We sorted a sack of rice by picking out any little stones or straws. The younger girls came home from school, dropping their satchels and letting their chadurs fall in a heap at their feet, they greeted me politely by saying, *'Salaam.'* The grandmother peeled an orange for them while they got out exercise books which opened from the right with a picture of the Shah. An ant crossing the carpet was intercepted by the youngest who took it on her hand. She watched the insect with an expression of listlessness, open-mouthed, hooded-eyes, her hair-ribbon loose, her long black hair tangled: she had a sallow strange face for a child. Pieces of orange were forced on me, (how could they eat if their guest didn't?) by the hospitable girls until I was nearly mad from continual light refreshment which killed my appetite for the gigantic meals that followed.

I helped thread the grandmother's lighter with a new wick. Proudly she smoked from a cigarette holder she had made. Did she buy the cloth? I think she did after pushing it away repeatedly so the saleswoman thought herself lucky to sell even at the lowest price. Grandmothers earned their position as heads of households.

I asked the girl who spoke French if I could go to the bazaar. 'Bazaar? Bazaar?' she replied, jolting her head as if it were the last place to go. However, they hid themselves in chadurs, warned me it would be, 'Dull, uncivilized and dirty,' and kindly took me.

Near the entrance goldfish were sold and plastic flowers, live peacocks and grapes and pears. We followed the passages of the souk to marvellous displays of polished samovars and carpets famous here for their vigorous colours. Another section sold Astrakan furs. I would have stayed hours had I not seen the girls were bored.

One morning I waited until the men of the house had gone to work and then crept to the gate and unbolted it. Tamar, in a fever of anxiety, held on to me. Although she called for help I got out before it came. Two minutes later she had collected chadur and slippers and came trotting after me. The faster I went, the faster she followed. People did stare at me. I leaped into a horse-cab. 'To the bus company.' I could say that. I had been cosseted long enough.

Tamar asked someone to telephone the son of the house at

his office. He drove to the bus company and arrived at the same time as I. 'Teheran,' I said weakly. He led me in and pointed to the reservation list, a front seat had been booked for me on the next bus, as I had asked. I was embarrassed. He drove me home. How could I face Tamar? I entered the house hoping she wouldn't hear. But there she was smiling and patting me on the back. She had come forward as if to take custody of me again, and I didn't mind at all.

For a farewell dinner the girl who spoke French invited me to her house. Their heating arrangement called a *corsi*, consisted of a charcoal brazier under a low, large table, covered by quilts and surrounded by pillows. One sat with legs and body submerged in warmth, head and shoulders resting on the cushions. There was room enough for everyone around it. 'What a good idea,' I said. The girl apologized; they were poor, they had no oil stoves, no wall-paper.

Dinner was served on a table cloth on the carpet. The ginger cat had a plate next to mine. Rice, lentils, spinach, stuffed aubergine, lamb and marmalade to end with, was our meal. Each person put his choicest piece of food on my plate. The servant had what we left, a beggar waiting outside the door ate her scraps. My journey to Teheran was discussed, *'Ish Allah,'* they said. You arrive if it is God's will. I agreed.

Sylvie Nisbet with Mount Arrat behind.

The Sphinx, Egypt.

A snake charmer at Luxor.

Another simple village.

The Magician, Mersire, Turkey.

A desert café.

Ispahan lady.

A poor catch.

Jerusalem priests.

The servant, Teheran.

An Iraqi band.

Istanbul mosque.

The bus.

Bus stop, Persia.

Bus stop, Jerusalem.

Sunrise, Masada.

Lunch, Masada.

Treasure.

Saturday, Masada.

Survivors of the storm, Masada.

Discovering The Hazar water shaft.

An Ending

The bus to Teheran left at dawn and my hosts had come to see me off. Penetratingly cold air made ice thick on the inside of the window. Where I breathed against the glass a pool of clarity formed, a minute later my view was again obscured. I waved goodbye quickly. Beside me a shrouded woman removed her shoes and sat on her feet to keep them warm. I did the same.

Our narrow route wound through hills. Several deserted lorries were covered by snowdrifts, others, smashed or upside down, had been pushed aside. A couple of buses going the opposite way were the only moving ones we passed, barely. A collision was narrowly avoided. One painted red and orange, the other salmon, purple and turquoise, enlivened the colourless landscape. Their engines made as much noise as aircraft taking off and why our driver couldn't deduce that something was coming around the corner, I didn't know. I no longer concerned myself with his disregard for danger. It was useless.

Zig-zagging slowly we reached the summit and the sun and a marvellous view of a rough white ocean of mountain tops. My neighbour handed me some sunflower seeds to nibble. The next vehicle could be seen kilometres away. Getting nearer it became obvious that one of us would have to draw aside to let the other pass. Passengers stood up to ascertain how much space would be left between bus and precipice. Persian music played deafeningly on the radio. Our driver had more nerve, going down hill he was going faster and probably couldn't stop anyhow. The other bus pulled aside at the last moment and our triumphant passengers let out a roar of approval as we shot by.

I shared my bread and cheese with my companion. 'English?' she asked. My admission pleased her. 'Me. Baby. Doctor. English.' We understood each other. She added excitedly, 'Me Russe!' I should have matched her patriotism. At a rest-stop a miserable snivelling creature barely covered in rags came out of a hole in the snow. Was this man a professional 'shiverer', a character similar to those described by Mayhew, the Victorian sociologist, in the London of a hundred and fifty years ago? The beggar cried so piteously, the Russian woman gave him all her small silver coins.

The WCs in these places, usually a hole in the ground with a makeshift screen around it, had minimal privacy, yet everyone was discreet. For the smallest tip, a blind or crippled man handed one a pottery flask of water which was used instead of lavatory paper. When I went to these WCs or even behind the bus all eyes were instantly averted.

The tea house was exactly like the last with its splendid portrait of the Shah. For an awful minute I thought there had been no progress. We all ate mounds of perfectly cooked rice. Every café provided the same food, had the same red plastic sugar bowls and similar pictures of a woman surrounded by doves, and fluffy kittens, or of roses and white horses in magenta moonlight, hanging on the walls. Their lush triteness hypnotized me. Automatically everyone prayed facing the direction of Mecca. How did they know the Holy City's location, indoors, outdoors, even on snowy, starless nights?

'Teheran by midnight,' the driver had promised but it was much later when we arrived. The Russian woman, met by her Persian husband, took me to their house for the remainder of the night. Tired, unthinkingly I brushed my teeth in their courtyard pool, a place reserved only for the ritual splashing of one's face. To my horror, even in the dark we could see my toothpaste foam floating out over the surface of the clear water. A number of such *faux pas* still cause me embarrassment when I remember them.

The following morning I transferred to a cold and expensive hotel. My visit to the Persian capital was brief because after seeing the museum and getting an impression of this fairly modern city, rebuilt after earthquakes, I found no reason to stay. I went on immediately to Isphahan, the town that became my favourite. Sufficiently far south to be mild in winter, a barrier of snow-capped mountains seemed also to keep at bay the hectic modernisation of Teheran. In Isphahan rich blue glazed mosque domes gleamed among a yellow ochre mass of low town buildings. I felt safe and peaceful there walking along the river in the early morning. The Persian poor, swaddled and bound up in felt rags, looked poorer here, and the rich richer than in any Arab country. No one was my equivalent. The poor reacted to my attention as if I were a lord and master. The rich found my by now dusty, scruffy clothes a betrayal of their proper standards. Tourists by the hundreds and their hotels I'm glad to have missed, despite the fact that I was more alone, more of a curiosity then I should have been. Until the snows melted only a trickle of water flowed in the wide river bed bordered by poplars, pickerers, washer-women and refuse dumps. Farther along by one of the ancient bridges a café served lettuce washed in the river (not a good idea) with olive oil, men sat about eating it. The limp leaves, the lethargic stream, the meditating Persians reflected my mood. I had nothing to do. Even in Mersine I had felt more alive than here.

The centre of Isphahan, Shar Abbas Square, at the time of Queen Elizabeth I had been a polo field. A hundred years ago a traveller found shops selling nightingales in the square. 'The birds are very sad in those hateful cages,' he recounts. Instead of a Persian carpet he had planned to get for himself, the writer buys and sets free a hundred of 'these poor little prisoners', only half a mile from their shop where the sharp-witted owner will catch them again the next day. We travellers can be as curious as the places we visit.

A big garden now fills the square and it was the gardeners' way of working that caught my attention. The gardeners started four in a line together, chanting, 'All-ah!' and they raised their hoes in unison. 'All-ah!' signalled all hoes lowered. 'All-ah!' as all hoes turned the earth. 'All-ah!' the procedure began once more with arms and hoes raised. A funeral march of productivity, I thought, but here a fair way to get work done. It was as though similar scenes recorded in Egyptian tomb paintings had come to life.

An ancient palace in the square with twelve wooden columns supporting a verandah and reflected in a pool was logically called the Palace of the Twenty Four Columns. Inside a honey-comb of rooms, passages, and twisting stairs suggested intrigue. Mosques in the square were being restored and I was asked not to enter. Women or perhaps any Western visitors were unwelcome then.

I ate a local speciality of finely sieved meat sprinkled with cinnamon, heated in butter and wrapped in paper-thin bread, Isphahan's hamburger, I suppose, and far more delicate than ours. The melons were famous for their 'special quality'. By law, fertilizer for the melon fields was contributed from everyone's WC. Daily hand-pulled carts collected the sealed containers left outside each house. I enjoyed these melons and only later learned the source of their sweetness.

For the first time I had come on holiday with a letter of introduction which I hoped relieved my mother's anxiety in my travelling alone. The letter was to an influential English couple but I was more interested in contacting my Northern hosts' cousin living in Shiraz. I travelled on, again by bus, to this southern town with its oranges and evergreens that vaguely recalled the Cote d'Azure.

The cousin met me. With black eyes and blank expression, he was polite and unintelligible. Conscientiously following his orders to look after me, he wore me out. My photographing servants or old things disgusted him to such an extent that I desisted. A child who started to clean my shoes unasked, he kicked in the face. He took me on a round of tea-drinking parties in large houses, belonging to large families. They offered me cakes, nuts and tea, then the same again at the next place. It was unforgivably bad-mannered of me even to hint of being bored, frustrated and fed-up. Sensitive to my reaction, the Persians laughed to cover their embarrassment, a type of laughter that is often heard and usually totally misinterpreted by foreigners.

While the cousin was taking an afternoon rest, I got away on my own to visit a Persian garden. Its formal walks, pools and waterfalls were not as exquisite as early Persian paintings had led me to expect. A policeman on duty in the garden followed me, saying correctly in English, 'This is a tree', 'this is water', 'this is a flower'. Desperate as he was to practise the language, he hadn't learned anything else and couldn't be dismissed or quietened. I left and walked back across the empty plain so vast I felt less than an ant. How could I ever travel across the world? By keeping going, was the answer. I did get back to my hotel but only by putting my head in a bucket of water did I revive. Was it sunstroke or circumstances that made me feel slightly demented?

The cousin caught a cold. This was my chance to go to Persepolis! I hired a vintage Alfa Romeo for the one hundred and twenty kilometre journey at the bargain price of one pound sterling. I was thrilled, then at the last minute the cousin recovered sufficiently to accompany me.

Every few kilometres the car stopped. I did not know the reason and because of the cousin's expression, I dared not ask. A soldier on a bicycle whom we had passed would again ride by. After our machine had a rest, we would start off in a burst of noise, smoke and speed, obliterating the cycling soldier. The cousin concluded our driver, an old man with an angelic smile and no concentration, smoked opium. Neither he nor the car was fit for the trip it seemed. The window had a way of opening slowly by itself. When it got nearly to the bottom, the cousin would shout an order for it to be closed, giving the driver such a fright his hands would jump off the steering wheel, his foot would press the accelerator to the floor, the car would cough, and once more come to a shuddering stand-still.

We picked up several passengers as angelic-looking as the driver. They had been sitting by discarded shovels along the road and were perhaps waiting for a bus? The cousin was too feverish to object to the old man's initiative and these unforeseen complications meant that we did not reach Persepolis until sunset.

This great palace and city backed by mountains had a magnificent setting overlooking the plain. The reliefs that remained in situ were beautifully preserved. I explored, with the place to myself, frantic in the fading light and as excited as a discoverer. A guide who merely recounted historical facts wouldn't have helped. I longed for someone who could make archaeology come alive, who, in a humanistic way, would teach me about the ancient inhabitants. The sort of experiences I had suited the sort of person I was. I believed if I could change life would become more rewarding, what I didn't know was how to bring this about.

I stayed until it was completely dark. The cousin spied on the driver, 'Smoking, just as I thought and not doing a stroke of work on the car!' Though our return was no quicker I was as content as could be, and the cousin slept.

The next morning an old man at a mosque door inscribing brass seals regarded me fiercely. I asked if I might take his photograph. For a whole minute he considered before saying 'No'. Then he smiled. He was willing to engrave my name on a seal in Persian for fourpence. Meanwhile the cousin had walked off into the distance. 'If you insist on doing terribly dangerous things, I am not going to stay with you,' he declared when I caught up with him. I apologized. What a pity it was my last day in Shiraz, not my first.

The bus to Teheran went by Persepolis in daylight so I could admire it again. Travelling by public transport I saw the country and made contact, I had no desire for the isolation and difficulties of my own car or the speed of an aeroplane.

That early morning our bus, going around an icy corner, overturned, or rather a tree saved it from falling completely on its side. A bus of the rival company, following close behind, hoping to overtake, skidded into ours. No one was hurt though passengers wailed loudly until they got out and realized they could still walk. I went on to the road to warn future traffic of the accident but, showing their concern for me, screeching women passengers dragged me back. Of course five minutes later a third bus, its driver staring at the scene, crashed into the mêlée. It was a herd of cows, also overturning on the icy corner, that finally caused laughter from the assembled seventy or eighty passengers and onlookers. The atmosphere relaxed, villagers came out in their pyjamas, a few shops opened for business. Drivers of rival bus companies shook hands and grinned. Soldiers with fixed bayonets arrived, and showed concern for the bent tree which 'belonged to the government'. Enough money was raised between the drivers to prevent the soldiers filing a report of the accident with the police. After this we set off with frequent calls to Mahomet, Ali and Allah at every corner, hill or hole in the road.

I returned from lunch at one of the road-side cafés and first noticed the elderly English woman sitting alone in the back of the bus. She held out some home-made cookies, which I accepted. 'I have lived here thirty years,' she was soon telling me, 'and I *never* go into these local cafés and I don't think you should either. Dirt and disease are everywhere.' Finally she introduced herself; she was the one person in the whole country to whom I had a letter of introduction. Although the letter was in the top pocket of my rucksack, I just went on eating her cakes and left it there.

I stayed in Teheran only long enough to acquire a return visa through Iraq and then once more I was on a bus again. All places taken, the engine started. Women gossiped across the aisles. The two opposite me had long upper lips and long, drawn-down noses. With lithe movements, wrapping their chadurs around them, talking with the corner held in their teeth, they smoked, with limp hands exposing the glittering gold of rings and many bracelets. At the first stop snowflakes fell, umbrellas were opened, horse-cab drivers shook themselves, and one tied his scarf with a tug. Their horses had hennaed manes. I got out and admired a butcher's stall where sliced oranges decorated the raw meat. Beggars pestered me, so into outstretched hands I put bread and dates which went straight into their mouths. They wouldn't ask again but looked hungrily at the little I had left for myself. Our driver returned carrying parcels, ridges of snow on either shoulder. Out of the village we overtook a caravan of two strings of laden, lurching, wet, grey camels, their drivers cowering under cloaks. An overturned lorry's load of turkeys had been released to scratch in the dirty snow. Mud was like waves when we drove through it. Shallow rivers had formed and had to be crossed quickly; there were no bridges.

Behind me an individual in a purple dressing-gown reclined on a double seat. Surrounded by gifts and cushions, he said, when I glanced around, 'I will talk to you.' I commented on the beauty of the silver birch trees and the mountains now we were leaving the snow. 'God sent you,' was his way of acknowledging my appreciation. He went on, 'The difference between our religions is that we do not turn the other cheek.' I didn't turn the other cheek either, I was going to say, when he handed me a raw onion and a piece of bread. Eaten together, they were remarkably refreshing. Something else to include in my essential travel equipment, I thought. Painting was the young man's hobby. He lived in Kadhmain the holy shrine outside Baghdad, and had been to London for an operation. 'Now we try prayer.' Where medicine had failed, he said, 'maybe faith works.' I noticed he was in pain. He invited me to visit his father's house in Kadhmain, 'We wait for you.' That night he stayed on his pile of pillows while I was swept along, with the women, to the hotel.

The hotel-owner had drooping moustaches, he sat cross-legged at the door in a fringed turban and silver embroidered lamb-skin coat. Hubble-bubble pipes hung along the whitewashed walls. Our driver, making a hole in the top of each raw egg, sucked up three which were served rolling on a small brass tray. We splashed our faces in the pool. Women with babies nursed them. Others prodded the mattresses for bugs. A boy ran in with a tiny clean mattress for me (on the orders of the invalid outside). Taking off my shoes and curling up I just fitted on it. Women leaned over me offering food, all their finger tips together, offering morsels of meat or fruit. In another instant I was asleep.

Crossing the high pass where the snow-covered mountain tops were illuminated by moonlight and shooting stars was special that evening. Afterwards the only time I talked about it, a girl in the room I did not know commented, 'Yes, I went the same way, by camel, when there was no moon. I was five, my brother three. They said they would have to kill him if he kept on crying. If we were heard or seen we would have all been killed.' The girl and her family were Jews who fled from Iraq to England.

As usual we left the hotel before sunrise. Nearing the Iraq frontier, a single approaching bus was the only thing to be seen on the horizon. When it passed us, it came so close the driving mirrors were shattered, showering those inside with fragments of glass that flew through the open windows. In the desert, to pass at top speed on an uneven track within a few centimetres of each other showed the skill of the rival company's drivers. Or did it? At the Iraq/Iran frontier a single wooden chair blocked the crossing point. No one smiled or said anything when I got out and photographed it.

I awoke in the English hostel in Baghdad to the greasy smell of bacon and frying bread. There was a sound of shoes marching about. Where were the thick carpets on which one sat or slept or ate? The room was cluttered offensively with ugly furniture. I had been six weeks away from the English and now, faced by them, found nothing to say. The clatter of cutlery from the dining room grated on my nerves. Those English women lacked both grace and sensitivity. Then I caught sight of myself in a mirror, tired, dirty, thin and as gauche as they.

Insmal, the hostel servant, must have lost half his Arab character through a life-time devoted to British cooking. The lunch he served of shepherd's pie and pudding could have come straight from an English boarding-school. In his Duke of Windsor checked trousers and black sweater he moved with a certain dignity, it was his permanently worried look and terribly lined face that betrayed the effort of loyalty to Europeans.

The gardener squatted, picking up every leaf fallen from the orange tree. He prayed in the rose garden and then lay in a half-rolled over position, an arm around his head, watching the watering system. A kite had caught in the telephone wires. The palms looked muzzy against the early sun. Cries of street-vendors sounded melodiously long. 'Ding. Ding. Ding,' the seller of paraffin came daily, hitting the tank behind his mule with a stick. The man on a camel selling salt came not as often. At *Poste Restante* I read and re-read my many letters. Friends could not imagine how much their words were appreciated here. I was satisfied by being remembered. I closed my eyes in the sun and thought about those who had written, more perhaps than I had when with them.

The windy night left telephone wires tangled and blew dates off the trees. The pungent smell of wet wool reached me before I saw the flock of sheep being driven across New Bridge. An angora goat among the bunch, terrified by city noise, started jerkily at every car. The flock, hearing their shepherd's shrill cry, trotted on, then lingered, nibbled rubbish in the gutter, chewed, and looked for more. The shepherd, cloak over his head, marched dutifully towards the market.

The atmosphere in Baghdad changed after the wind and rain. For a few hours no dust hung in the air, visibility was remarkable. Clean blue or gold domes shone gloriously. Garbage, floating in the Tigris, showed how quickly the river moved. Scribes were busy in the post office, soldiers with fixed bayonets looked rather surly. I expected politeness from every Arab. Rudeness was more serious than it would be in Europe. Sometimes we can't be bothered to be polite; here, bad manners implied a conscious insult.

I had postponed visiting Christopher for fear he had changed in the three years since we had met. 'Am I interrupting?' I asked as I walked into his office.

'No,' he sighed. 'How are you?' He had been trying to read the New Testament in Arabic. His quizzical expression, dry sense of humour and helpfulness were exactly the same. I could use a flat, he told me, until the new tenant, a friend of his, arrived from England. Christopher would send his driver to pick up my luggage. I wondered if it was only when someone like me barged in and asked questions that Christopher came out of his own world? He always made me welcome, yet I was an intruder.

From the window of my new flat I watched the sun set. A boy rode one of three cows he was taking home. Bats darted about madly. Smooth American cars sailed up and down the dirt road, tooting. I couldn't tell if they were taxis; everyone drove noisily. Too content to go to bed, I rearranged the rugs and listened to an old radio Christopher had lent me.

I awoke late, a sliver of sun as positive as a piece of cheese showed through the curtains. Unable to get up, I reached from my bed to pull them aside but they were stuck and a lizard fell upon me from the folds. Sun on the yellow-brick house next door made my eyes ache. Even the silence hurt. Entombed, I hated the blank blue sky. I was very ill.

Christopher must have come during the second or third day while I was asleep. A bag of oranges had been left outside my door and a piece of paper, to attract my attention, underneath. I tried to eat an orange every few hours and pulled my mattress into the sun on the balcony to get warm. Another day or two went by before I could drag myself downstairs. Taking a shoe to hammer on his door, I went to the ground floor flat inhabited by an elderly Englishman who, Christopher had informed me, taught English to the Arabs. Perhaps he would lend me a stove or get me milk?

'Come in!' a voice shouted, 'It's not locked.' The man was sitting in a chair surrounded by empty or half-empty bottles of whisky. 'Got that bloody Asian flu. You have too, by the look of you,' he shouted. For something to say, I asked the time. 'It's stopped. It won't do you the slightest good to know. There are half a dozen clocks, they've all stopped. Ha, ha.' I climbed the stairs on all fours, very slowly, back to my room.

The next morning the Englishman from downstairs shouted through my door, 'Christopher came. He said he thought you were dead. I said you weren't. Ha, ha. Want some Scotch?' His voice made me want to escape. I had a shower. I was recovering. Unfortunately, the food I bought stuck in my throat, the milk I drank greedily made me sick. No cure came as quickly as I wished.

A letter/card, a single sheet of folded paper awaited me at *Poste Restante* with the news that the young man on the bus had died of cancer in Kadhmain. His parents had dictated the letter to an Indian scribe at their son's request. He had waited in vain for my visit, it said. His death saddened me deeply yet I replied with trite phrases. So intent was I to get from place to place, I had ignored the seriousness of his illness. What was being revealed was too harsh to think about. How could I admit that my friends were acquaintances, that I loved no one, that no one loved me?. The daughter/parent relationship with which I had come into the world was the only one I knew. I was skiing all the time, even here, over the surface of life: I didn't know how to respond. I wasn't *able* to care. I could not cope. I closed my mind. I looked eagerly for ways of keeping busy.

Christopher and his wife made an effort to stay in touch with me now. They took me to a private view of paintings by Iraqi artists and a few days later invited me on a picnic. Why did we need guns? They were automatically included with blankets and tins of water and petrol. Christopher wearily explained. 'Plates!' I exclaimed, 'What do we need plates for?' Christopher's wife just looked at me and continued to wrap each one in a page from *The Observer*. We were not ready until after the sun had risen, reducing in my mind an adventure to a mere excursion. 'Why have a few houses the letters D.D.T. painted on them?'

105

'To show they have been fumigated,' Christopher muttered. We had not reached the desert and already the sun was hot.

'There's a fox in that wheat,' I observed.

'Yes, I saw him. Shoot.' As his wife had the picnic basket on her lap, I obediently let the gun go 'bang'. The jeep's wheels started to spin in a hollow, muddy from the last rain. By the time we manoeuvred to higher ground, the fox was well away.

No sooner had we chosen a place for lunch and started unpacking than Arabs appeared from an empty landscape. I did not like eating, almost could not by now, without sharing our food. Christopher just gave them cigarettes saying that was all they came for, and 'to look at my women'.

Lunch over, Christopher drove wildly, swerving as if to recreate the thrills of the last hunt, although we saw no game. Round and round a freak lake we went, only frightening the ducks from one side to the other. Back on a muddy track the wheels again spun and slithered: on and on we went. Christopher noticed an eagle perched on a mud-brick ruin. 'I could get him,' he declared.

'What, from here? Shoot it?' I questioned.

'Yes,' said Christopher grimly. At the first shot the eagle toppled off and vanished behind the wall. We drove over. The eagle stood in a corner with its back to us. Christopher went in and shot it twice more. Then the great bird, lying on the ground, wings fully out-stretched, the end feathers curling slightly, raised its head and looked up at the sky with a look of pure longing.

Christopher's wife turned away; covering her face with her hands, she moaned, 'He's not dead! He's not dead!' Her tears poured through her fingers. Christopher lifted his rifle butt. We left the scrunching noise.

'I shot him three times, I can't understand it.' He started the jeep with a roar. His wife did not say a word the whole way home.

I borrowed their cook's bicycle and shopping basket, and wearing old jeans, a *keffyeh* wrapped around my head with only eyes showing, I could have been an Arab. The freedom to look without being stared at gave me a sense of exhilaration. One policeman, curious why, on a warm morning, anyone should be so wrapped up, did watch me. I pedalled about joyfully, visiting many new places. Two Americans photographing from New Bridge offered an opportunity for me to check my disguise. Getting off my bicycle I approached them. 'Baksheesh,' I whined, 'alms for the love of Allah!' I insisted, holding out my sunburned hand. In unison they snapped their cameras shut and retreated. They had not even looked at me.

Full of confidence, after a few days I set out for Kadhmain. Europeans were not welcome there. An American photographer, it was said, determined to take pictures inside the mosque, was literally torn to pieces by the infuriated crowd. Two versions of the story existed, however: one said a little finger was recovered, another 'not even a little finger'.

I bicycled towards Kadhmain, feeling relaxed at last. The gold mosque dome glinted through the palms. In the village's many unpaved streets, thick mud remained. I skidded, got off and pushed. An Arab in the crowd suddenly steadied himself by putting his arm around my shoulder. Fear chilled me, my knees, though I kept on walking, were like jelly. Finding I was a good prop, he let me support him the length of the street. It was a vegetable market and may have been full of friendly shoppers rather than religious fanatics, but by the time I got away from him, I was shaking violently. The parents of the young man who died would have welcomed me, yet fear of emotional involvement led me from one lonely encounter (like this) after another.

From then on I spent the days lying by the American Embassy pool with other European girls. Only my walk to *Poste Restante* took me into town. On New Bridge one morning, traffic jammed the road in both directions. Drivers, leaving their cars where they were, had gone to the rail and were looking into the water. Someone had just jumped over. I slipped out of my coat and shoes in case the person needed help. My action was automatic. In the turbulent water I saw no one. Then I began to feel enraged by the onlookers who brushed their hands together with a that's-that gesture. I stood there, sickened by the incident, sickened by those around me. 'It is the will of God,' a spectator repeated. He *wanted* me to understand. With the same hand-brushing movement he dismissed the life that had been lost. Afterwards I couldn't stop crying. It was curious, on the departing bus, as we drove into the desert, I raised my head for the last sight of Baghdad and still in tears, saw other passengers were looking at me and weeping too.

* * *

I had woken with one thought: today I'm going home. The notice on the Paris station of St Lamare read: 'Passengers to England the front of the train only'. I climbed the train steps. My seat was hard and in a *Fumeura*, and the carriage much too hot. Yesterday's rain had recommenced before the pavements dried.

I took off my shoes. What a long trip it had seemed. During the crossing I slept a bit until the white cliffs came into view, then yellow sand, then emerald grass, finally we passed the pier. Customs men rubbed chalk on the bags and I settled on the London train with tea and fruit cake. A girl in the compartment talked about 'the importance of getting out of a rut', while in silence I watched the suburbs speed by.

I stopped in Victoria station's first telephone box, because of the Easter holiday most of my friends were away. My parents were in America. I rang my aunt. 'Usually you are back about this time,' she commented and invited me for a drink on Friday, a week away. 'Wear jeans if you like, darling. Just be yourself,' she added, slight apprehension in her voice.

'I'm glad you got back safely.' The tall bearded artist from across the road was walking his dog. 'I suppose you've, as they say, spent all your money?'

'Yes, I have!' He laughed at the joke. He was so rich that such things didn't happen to people he knew. Actually, my remaining thirty-five shillings was enough to last me until I earned more. What fascinated me about money was the making of it. If money had been given to me, it would have lost its allure.

'But didn't you know? William is in prison,' the girl said *sotto voce*. I had run into her in Brompton Road. 'He was taken there with the Ban the Bomb protesters when they were arrested.' She continued after a sigh, 'He seemed rather depressed. I visited them. They all wear uniforms. He has the privilege of doing some gardening but all the same I think he will be glad when he gets out.' We had brought a pint of milk and I had asked her up to the flat that I shared with several other girls. She drank a glass of milk and took some pills. 'I haven't seen you for so long,' she said, 'I hate to lose touch.' Then she sat there despondently with nothing more to say.

'You really went all that way?' My landlady couldn't believe it. 'Oh dear, that reminds me. A foreign gentleman rang you. I couldn't catch his name. Now who could that be? Can you guess?' Her little boy was full of news of Batman.

'He has magic in him. I had a mouse once with magic in him. I said "abracadabra" and he disappeared, forever.' He told me about his school lunches of pilchards, potatoes and greens cooked until they had neither taste nor colour. I said, 'It was the same in my day.'

'Was it?' he asked incredulously. I told his mother how glad I was to be back, to cook my own meals, to sleep in my own bed, to see familiar faces not just strange ones. Her little boy whispered, 'It's going to be a wonderful summer, you won't have to go away again. It's going to be so hot people will drop dead with heat. The paper said so.' Meanwhile Easter was cold. The trees were in bud, waiting.

'Welcome home, darling!' cried the man in my life, laughing. I envied his easy enjoyment of life. I had tried to avoid meeting him. The sight of him made me dizzy with longing. There were never days off, never times I could think 'pooh, what's so special about him?' The first time we met he told me, 'I can't play tennis awfully well but I'm marvellous in bed.' A pathetic cliché, I supposed. Long distance telephone calls, discarded women's clothes, numerous *objets d'art*, produced an indiscriminate, overwhelming, impersonal atmosphere in his flat. He had got me drunk before kissing me. I tried to leave, unsteadily.

'I'm too drunk to make love to you, it could be anyone.'

'You kill me!' He had a loud laugh.

I longed for him to hold out his hand, for any sign of tenderness. He never would. 'Don't be complicated. Don't be sentimental,' those were his instructions. My demanding from someone something he didn't want to give was poisonous, but then, I understood nothing. I could not have imagined that in a few years' time, when I was happily settled down, we would be 'just' friends.

Afterwards, he despised women, afraid they wouldn't go. I could hardly leave quickly enough. Even meeting him in the street, as I just had, gave me a haggard look. It should have been a good relationship, instead it was a sick one. Certainly I could see my mistake. And he would often give me the right advice. 'Find someone else!' he would cry if I complained at all. My remarks infuriated him. He preferred me silent. He tried asking for things, money or more whisky.

'I won't give you anything,' I said. Except myself. Trusted, adored, talked to, I wanted to be, and at night alone in this cold and lonely flat I would scream into my pillow for him.

When people said to me, 'You have so many friends,' I wanted to ask,

'Is your happiness as precarious as mine? Do most of you live on the edge of sadness?'

I must cure myself, I thought, only whole people are wanted in this world. On my next holiday I would stay away longer. I couldn't go back to Baghdad. Perhaps I should start with two weeks in Israel. It looked like such a small country, though. Where would I go after that?

To be occupied, to be cheerful, 'to get out of yourself' (the advice my landlady always gave us), I walked over to see Fiona. Her flat was rather claustrophobic, at the top of a flight of dark stairs. She opened the door cautiously and seemed pathetically pleased it was me. In baggy red jeans, a clashing red cashmere sweater and pearls, she looked older than I remembered. Had I too aged that much without noticing? The biscuits tasted dusty, the tea made with a used bag at least wasn't too strong. I sat on the carpet and by leaning against a tall bookcase accidentally dislodged the largest book balanced on top. The *Seven Pillars of Wisdom* crashed down, barely missing me. Her old cat lying by me, that looked and acted like a stuffed one, didn't turn a hair. (I picked it up by the tail once to see if it had any reactions. It hadn't much.)

Fiona began by telling me about her latest holiday in

110

Morocco. 'The hotel boys, the shepherds, the souvenir sellers, I felt at home among them. You know, Lawrence says you can never change the colour of your skin, your blood, your nature, but I feel quite happy among the Berbers, one of them, virtually.'

'It's a great discovery,' I answered, 'though the final realization is, I think, that you will find Lawrence right.' She did not believe me. Every year Fiona's flat was filled with more from the Moroccan souks. I was glad, anyhow, her pretty china tea cups had not yet been swapped for glasses. Would she one day swap everything, and after one holiday not return? Would she grow old and grand, holding court among her Arabs? We search for appreciation and perhaps that's what Fiona lacked in England.

I got back only to be telephoned by the man in my life. I didn't answer. He hung up. Being unloved by him made me want to die. Does this wish sound exaggerated? Because of its truth, I can say that I thought more and more about suicide. Day followed day with a sort of downhill momentum. Friendships seemed hollow. My existence proved my mediocrity. How absurd that we are judged or remembered for our work when the only thing that matters is how well we live. 'Never met anyone like you before who could be, and liked being, alone,' was his explanation of my attraction. I did not tell him it was worse loneliness, being with him.

Already I longed for another holiday on this, the first weekend of being back in London.

Masada

Though it was only a grey strip of land in the grey sea that dawn, the North African refugees wept at their first sight of Israel. I stared overboard with apprehension caused by any foreign country new to me. I noticed hills, then houses, and could pick out their details as we sailed slowly nearer. I would feel all right once we had landed, I told myself. A sophisticated New York couple at the ship's railings discussed their proposed tour of the country in a blasé manner but as we docked in Haifa they too had tears in their eyes. The woman turned to me, 'You can't imagine what it is like to see so many Jews. Look at the people on the quay, the police, the customs officers, the drivers, they're Jews, they're *friends.*'

To begin my visit to Israel I had volunteered to work at a remote archaeological site called Masada near the Dead Sea. A man in the station from whom I asked directions, advised me to catch an express to Tel Aviv, there I could get a bus for the last part of the trip. I had no Israeli currency so he changed a couple of dollars for me and I bought a ticket as the train came.

Soldiers, young men and women, occupied most of the seats. I found the station austere, (not by Middle Eastern standards, already I was using European ones). Sand dunes and the sea bordered one side of the railway line and on the other, small houses in fields were perhaps a kibbutz? Soon I saw the apartment buildings of Tel Aviv. The elderly business man who had directed me to the right train now went out of his way to show me the Beersheva bus as if he were a friend who had come to help me.

The bus roared off immediately. Everything moved in this

country! I looked out of the window at the cultivated landscape and noticed what could be done in this part of the world by hard work and by controlling flocks of goats. A family next to me invited me to stay with them after I had been to Masada. They wrote out their address and instructions to get there. People acted as if they knew me, I thought.

I soon found our meeting place in Beersheva. It was in the public gardens that the Masada volunteers had been instructed to assemble. Already a bearded man lay on the grass by a rucksack and a few people with suitcases sat on a wall. An old man in a bright smock talked animatedly, he was a French 'naturalist'.

For the two hour drive to the site we travelled in closed lorries, canvas flaps over the back kept out the cold and hid the scenery. When we stopped and got out, when I first saw the flat-topped rock of Masada looming above us and the Dead Sea nearby, I loved the dramatic landscape. I expected a great adventure. A young Israeli physicist who had sat by me during the drive began to lead our group up the steep winding trail, aptly called the Snake Path, to the top.

Herod fortified Masada by building cisterns, store rooms and palaces in case he needed a sanctuary. After his death in 4 BCE, a small Roman garrison was kept on at the fortress. Two years after the destruction of their temple in 70 BCE the Jews revolted and a group of more than 960, known as Zealots, by surprising the Roman garrison, captured Masada for their own refuge. The Roman 10th Legion led by Flavius Silva was dispatched to lay siege and quell the uprising. Not until a ramp had been constructed on the western side, walls broken and all hope lost did the Jews choose suicide as free men rather than life as slaves of the Romans. Because of the heroism of Masada's last defenders the site became a place of pilgrimage. Our camp, like that of the Roman's commander's, was situated on the western side and by walking up and over Masada upon our arrival, we got an idea of the site's strategic significance.

The physicist went back to carry a girl with an asthma attack. The climb sorted out the fit from those in not such good condition among the young, the old, the Jew, the non-Jew, students or businessmen who had come on two weeks'

113

leave. Although not used to a spartan life the majority adapted quickly.

I went ahead with the old man, the 'naturalist', who found climbing easy. A black nose protruded from the brief-case he carried (a truck had taken our luggage to the camp), and on top, waiting for the last of the climbers, he opened it, 'Oh my God, she's had puppies!' He replaced the two mouse-sized creatures he had found, while the mother, after a run, jumped in again of her own accord.

We crossed the top of Masada, a plateau of about twenty acres, roughly the shape of a ship and then saw the Roman siege ramp, a huge structure of earth, rocks and wooden beams, as I noticed later. The ramp provided the easiest access, elsewhere the cliff had a steep drop. The Jewish defenders must have felt secure at the beginning, then dismayed as they saw the ramp being constructed, the battering ram being hauled into place, and finally desolate when the walls were breached. It was on that last night the Jews drew lots to kill each other before the Romans entered.

The sun had set and below Masada, in our camp, I looked up at the dark shape of the mountain. Romans, too, had looked up from there. The physicist was walking with me towards our tents and I asked him, 'Doesn't Masada make you sad?'

'No!' The answer from this the first Israeli I had met shot back like a challenge. 'It makes me proud.' He left me, aware of a vital world to which he belonged. I felt I had the inadequacy of a schoolgirl then.

I chose a bed by the entrance of a tent already inhabited by Israeli and English girls, eight in all. 'The stores', was where I would begin work the next day. 'You're lucky. You don't find much but the view is lovely,' a Kensington girl told me. 'I work in the casement wall, we find lots,' she said. I asked what the archaeologists were like. 'Pro-British. You sift, the boys dig,' she added.

We climbed Masada at dawn. Our area looked a gloomy prospect. Outlines of corridor-like rooms, closed at one end, ran parallel to each other. These stores built by Herod had contained stocks of food and arms for ten thousand men. The walls, destroyed by an earthquake, were being restored by

114

experts not only to show this important aspect of defence but also to clear the ground of fallen debris so we could dig. A wilderness, a dusty pile of rubbish it seemed to my untrained eye. How could it be sorted out? Two of us sifted buckets full of earth over a wheelbarrow. Earth fell through leaving stones and perhaps a few pieces of pottery on the top. I saw a coin, it was easy: the metal had turned bright green. Then I had a moment of doubt, could I be the first to touch this coin lost by someone nearly two thousand years ago? Our archaeologist came over, he said tenderly, 'Yes, it's a coin. It's beautiful!' I was thrilled and immensely encouraged. Only later I learned he had found hundreds of these little ones.

After a few days the weather became colder and at the 9.30 breakfast I lay down in our trench out of the wind. A jagged piece of pottery stuck in my back. I turned over and saw it was covered with writing. 'How did you find it?' our archaeologist questioned me. Would he understand? It found me.

Then the professor appeared, 'Good,' he said, 'try to find the rest. It is freshly broken so the other pieces have to be here. No matter how little they are keep them.' I recognized Professor Yadin from his photograph in newspapers, what the pictures had not revealed was his great presence and authority which, combined with a kind manner and tone of voice made me want to do my best.

I wrote home that night. 'We have found several ostricans. One imagined the person who lost the coin but the writing and reading of a word on the pottery was a much more personal contact with the past.' Living in Masada, removed from our age of television and cars, even from trees and houses, I became sensitive to the life and problems of those who had been there 1900 years ago. I wanted to remain longer than the two weeks for which I had been accepted. Would my luck continue? Would the archaeologists let me stay?

I didn't mind sifting but I didn't like the implication I was capable of nothing else. A pick axe was not so heavy, finding walls not so difficult. I began by cleaning a row of stones. To the architect I announced, 'A wall.' With a tap of his hammer he brought it down. After a while I learned to recognize real ones: the human processing that had gone into their construction spoke to me.

The subtleties of an earth floor took longer to identify. By watching our archaeologist, an artist in using tools. I understood the importance of neatness and order. He made his tools work while I had been lumbered with them. This young man hod not only had to supervise his whole area of the excavation but tie ropes around volunteers working near the edge, trace missing sandwiches and settle petty disputes. He was fair and patient, and how he remained so for two long winters, I don't know.

If there had been many levels of occupation volunteers might have missed them. As it was groups removed top soil and experienced workers cleared the floor. Masada was a fortress designed for Herod and his bodyguard, not for the many Zealot families who took over, making their homes in the casement walls by putting up partitions or camping in the palace. Their *mickvas,* ritual baths, and their restoration of the synagogue, among other things, proved how deeply religious they were. Column sections taken from Herod's northern palace made convenient tables and we found many of these stones in secondary use. One of the Zealots' pools or ovens might be built against a frescoed wall, or it might cover part of a smart mosaic floor. The emphasis on luxury during the first occupation changed to a struggle for survival during the second.

So well did the dry climate preserve olive and date stones, the volunteers who found them thought their fruit must have been eaten this season. Glass, copper, wood, leather, mosaic, fresco, bone, we learned to identify materials and then the Hebrew word for each. Rope had to be removed delicately. Burned roof beams, evidence of the Zealots' destruction of their own homes before the Romans' entry, had to be photographed. A stylus, a ring, a key, helped us to imagine former residents. One room we called 'Joseph's'. Curtain rings made us wonder about his interior decoration. Then I found what I thought were two of his teeth. 'Goats' teeth!' our archaeologist retorted.

From rims and bases of the functional pottery we found, we were taught to visualize the whole pot. It was the humble possessions (half buried by a Zealot in the last hour of his life) that had significance at Masada.

The loudspeaker did not wake us on Shabat. We could

sleep late. A walk was planned and this week it was to be a tour of the Roman siege forts. I needed time to look around. Being here was an extraordinary experience, an isolated incident in my life, it had no connection with what had come before, nor I thought, what would follow.

One evening in the dining tent I sat next to the expedition's photographer. Discovering I liked the artist, he described a Kokochka he had owned in Czechoslovakia. The Germans had come and he had fled for his life, 'Leaving everything behind,' as he put it, though his enthusiasm and zest for life made him seem enriched beyond measure.

After work we raced for a hot shower. If the men got there first, they had their showers before us. Girls cleaning pottery in the base camp tried to reserve the showers, then the men had the idea of coming in anyhow. 'We don't mind sharing,' was their reaction. So we often bathed late, in luke-warm water.

The wind raged all night and the next morning we found our tin shack WCs had been blown fifty metres down the wadi. Then carpenters secured the little huts, the wind ripped off all the doors. One volunteer who dropped his transistor down our WC, where it played for three days, was famous for that alone. Waiting outside once I grew bored and hurled a large rock onto the WC's tin roof. The professor, unperturbed, stepped out and continued on his way without a comment or look in my direction. He knew it was unnecessary.

During the dark January and February mornings we sometimes had to wash our faces in the pouring rain under a tap from which the water was blown horizontally. However, the life suited me. If one went to bed early (except when the professor gave a lecture) one was ready to wake at the loudspeaker's Hebrew 'good morning'. I liked being first at breakfast and sitting over my hot coffee for five minutes. The man who handed out cutlery at the dining tent entrance, twisted the cheap spoons and forks into fantastic shapes. It would have been one of these I would have taken if I had kept any Masada souvenirs. The man always laughed and talked to everyone in Hebrew though at that time all I could say in his language was, 'Where is my wheelbarrow?'

Our food arrived by truck from Arad, the nearest village. If our evening meal was late we stood watching the hills anxiously. Once all the bread bounced out leaving a trail of loaves along the desert track. Except for some cheese in the lunch sandwiches, cheese resembling plaster of Paris, food was plentiful and good. Soup, brown rice, meat balls, egg salad and fruit was a typical supper that first year. I was always hungry especially if cold weather and hard work coincided. Curiously enough others didn't often finish their food. One lucky day I counted the number of bread-slices I'd scrounged and eaten: twenty-five.

The sun rose over the mountains of Moab across the Dead Sea. The sea could be as grey, shiny and sinister as snake skin, or as colourless and dull as its name implied, or even bright blue with Mediterranean movement and white caps. Opposite Masada a sand bank called The Tongue extended, where supposedly, the Dead Sea was shallow enough to cross to Jordan by camel. Except for a few lights at night I noticed no sign of life from the Arab villages. I often thought about former holidays; being able to participate in this excavation provided a better introduction than I had had to any other country.

A soldier who had escaped as a child from the Warsaw ghetto, worked with us. 'Israelis don't know what it is like to walk down the street with people yelling at them, "Jew!" "Jew!" To them it's a compliment!' He talked as if words were bursting from him; he bombarded me. He had lost his whole family in Poland.

One woman who sang as she worked had survived a concentration camp. A man who joined our group had a finger shot off by the British as he was crawling up a beach after fleeing Germany and landing 'illegally' in Palestine. He had pretended to be dead and was added to a pile of corpses. 'And look, I'm here!' How could I admit to these people that only a month ago I had been fed up with life? What would they think if they knew petty problems made me suicidal? The soldier from Warsaw advised intuitively, 'Don't make feeling sorry for us an extension of your own self-pity.' We had an affair. It made me happy. For him it was nothing. I tried to hide my enthusiasm. We drifted apart.

The monk in our team was a good sport. Eventually he wore shorts for work. During six weeks he carried buckets and emptied our wheelbarrow with exceptional willingness while having to put up with bad language, companions who did not share his convictions and, at night, a noisy tent. If the wind was not too strong he held mass in the wadi. One girl attended. He had taught himself thirteen languages. I used to listen to him re-telling the same joke in half a dozen of them for our linguistically mixed team. If we met on the way to the WC in the evening he would stop a minute and point out stars with his torch. When he left he gave me a tin of apple sauce he had brought with him for a special occasion. The monk used to relax on a rock shaped like a chaise longue every morning at break time and I had only to catch sight of this place, on later visits, to visualize him there. My Masada was full of ghosts, living and dead.

A phenomenal success was the 'Liar', an American boy with an innocent face. After carefully studying his audience he would tell the most wildly credible lie he could imagine. The Queen was expecting a child. 'She's had twins!' he shouted, rushing into a susceptible 'English' tent. The story spread, it was not doubted. Days later the correct news of a single child reached us and was disbelieved. To prove his skill he caught me with the story that Ringo Starr had been killed in a car crash. This Beatle was my favourite and I was upset. Little English girls were the easiest victims. I remember their throwing down tools, crawling out of trenches, jumping walls and deserting our area as if it were a sinking ship in order the see the latest arrival. The 'Liar' described a helicopter's landing which he could see from his position on top of a high tripod. 'And Princess Margaret steps down, smoothing her gloves. She is wearing a pastel blue . . . .' I looked at him in amazement. Perched on the second tripod myself, I could see only the professor getting out, wearing jeans and a plaid shirt. That happened on the Liar's first day at Masada. The next he was transferred to work in another area much to my disappointment.

We were a good team until, on one two week cycle, a volunteer arrived who expected personal credit. 'I found this.' 'I found that,' he kept crying. Certainly we boasted of being the best team while knowing that any one of us could have achieved nothing without the others. After getting an Israeli to write in ancient Hebrew, 'You are a donkey', on a piece of pottery, I planted it. '*I* found an *ostrican!*' The volunteer went prancing off to our archaeologist who for about two seconds was pleased, then they were both very angry with me.

So many volunteered that there were not places enough for half of them. I longed to be worthy of staying yet I still did things I shouldn't. 'Here we work not with passion but with love,' the oldest archaeologist warned me to no avail. I was intolerant of those who did not enjoy the excavation as much as I. It took me a long time before I learned how to share my appreciation with people instead of criticizing, to understand that they too responded to care and patience in the field just as I had. The professor observed, 'Some people need Masada more than Masada needs them.' In my case I was determined to make it mutual and went whirring on. They must have had pity; they let me stay.

One night rain pounded the tent, lightning flashed, half an hour later a terrific wind turned its force on us. I got up and tied my packed belongings to the bed. The next morning all was quiet and warm. Sheep-faced I undid the string. It was Shabat. I sunbathed. Our washing fluttered on the line, flowers were coming up, dragon-flies, bees and butterflies soared out on their first flight. The air was so clear and still I heard the footsteps of someone climbing Masada a kilometre away. From that day onward I no longer slept (for warmth) under my mattress but on it.

I looked forward to receiving letters even though one friend wrote only about her cat. A snow scene postcard from another I hung over my bed. My mother sent me a packet of mosquito repellant. I had not told her about our 'Two Step Snake' as an Israeli called it. 'That's how far you get after it's bitten you,' he said. Was he joking?

Everyone had gone away for the weekend. Only a Swiss girl and I were left in our tent so we gave it a good cleaning and when the job was done she shared some chocolate with me. A few crumbs must have dropped to the ground because a jerboa shot out from under a bed and devoured them instantly. Desert rats were equally tame. Even though I shouted, two had gone on chewing my rucksack and were only stopped by a neighbour's throwing hot tea over them.

120

One archaeologist collected live scorpions and supplied us with glass jars to catch them. 'At this time of year they are a bit slow but be careful when they begin to wake up.' These desert creatures preferred shade, not knowing that, I killed a baby scorpion by putting it, in its jar, in the sun.

A Dane, ravenously hungry, one evening, complained. 'A crow carried away my sandwich at lunch time.' In our normal lives we kept creatures under control, here, I felt, it was their domain. Only mosquitoes were absent.

I should have learned Hebrew but at Masada just a few sentences were essential such as, 'I want my egg hard/soft boiled.' 'Please,' and 'Thank you' are vital words in other countries, once learned in Israel, one learned to forget them. Everyone is close and those two words are understood. One *knows* that if something is needed badly enough it will be given, at least this is my personal experience. Anywhere else perhaps kindness, hospitality and consideration couldn't be given and received so simply. Now if an Israeli says, 'Please', or 'Thank you' to me, I feel vaguely disconcerted. I'm told I've been lucky, that's the way my life is.

Interested visitors often came to note the excavation's progress. During the last rain of winter we scrambled out of our trench to meet one of these escorted groups. Black mud covering us made us as approachable as primaeval reptiles. The professor had with him a man with whom he was discussing the area. Then he introduced us volunteers by name (how did he remember?) and we gave welcoming smiles. The guest actually came forward to shake our filthy hands. Who could be that diplomatic, I wondered. 'The British Ambassador,' the professor introduced his guest in turn.

Archaeologists went home for Shabat, most volunteers rushed off sightseeing while I was content to stay in a camp filled, at this time of year, with the scent of flowering bushes. For a few weeks the desert was tinged with green before every plant disappeared. Seemingly dead stalks burst with cactus-like leaves, the pollen of tiny flowers dyed my feet yellow. A desert rat leaped into his burrow and then could not resist returning so when I put my face at his level he backed up a centimetre and eyed me beadily. An eagle remained standing on its rock as I walked by. A young camel

121

enjoyed being scratched behind its ears. Those Shabats were unforgettably peaceful.

Josephus in his *History of the Jews* describes the fortifications at Masada and through the witness of two women and their children who hid at the time, the Zealot's mass suicide. I read about Herod's life while actually in his northern palace, seeing the view he saw: a dark patch to the north, the oasis of En Gedi, once belonged to Cleopatra. From where I sat one looked in the direction of Jerusalem, here many other in the past had watched and waited for reinforcements or for news.

Soon the grass burned away and the flowers vanished, only a few bushes remained green at the bottom of the wadi. Shortly after dawn the heat became intense. It was Passover. Work stopped and everyone had gone home except some soldiers and three of us who volunteered to guard the site. No visitors could be admitted on their own until Masada was officially opened to the public.

I kept guard at the edge of the rock where there was a slight breeze. The other English volunteer on duty stood at the top of the Snake Path with a pick axe. 'It gives one *some* sort of authority,' he explained. When a party of thirty Israeli policemen came up he recounted, 'I told them all to sit and they sat, I was so amazed, I could hardly believe it. They waited while I telephoned the office for confirmation. Told they must leave, they left!'

To be visited out here was an event. I wished I could be a guide instead of a guard. Few tourists whom we had to chase away would have done any harm but they could have fallen into a cistern. Until ropes were put up and paths laid out, site and sightseers were equally hazardous to each other. I found one unauthorized visitor, the large plumber, hiding behind a small pile of stones who claimed he was entitled to see the place because he had repaired our water pipe. On another occasion five parachutists climbed the very difficult southern end of Masada, fully armed. They were amused when I presented myself in shirt and bathing suit as the guard. The only way to stop them was to say I was doing what I could for Israel even though it was just sitting there and asking people to leave as the professor instructed, while they had the privilege of walking around the desert in the terrible heat with all their equipment to do their part in protecting Israel. Meekly they left and filed down the Snake Path.

From my vantage point I could see the rabbi walking out of camp, not wanting to wait for a lift on Sunday. He had walked here though we had made the three-hour drive over difficult western track to collect him from Beersheva. Young soldiers, who had been models of perfection up to then, were full of foolish high spirits during the Seder. The rabbi had ignored them and carried on. The mood of camp lacked co-ordination now that nothing except boredom threatened them.

* * *

The first Masada season came to an end and I caught the 5 a.m. bus from Beersheva to Eilat, a southern town on the Red Sea. Occasionally we made a detour to deliver post or passengers to desert kibutzim with their swimming pools, deck chairs on lawns, flowering mimosa trees and modern sculpture. Then back we went to the rocky landscape, thorn bushes and camels. Our driver was armed, our feeling was of once more being in the wilds.

At the half-way café water sprayed onto the corrugated roof dripped off its edges cooling the air and making the soothing noise of rain. Between the café and our bus the awfulness of the heat hit me again. A beatnik girl passenger removed her long Bedouin dress, she travelled the rest of the journey towards the sea in her bathing suit. Our route ran parallel to the Amman/Aqaba road down which a Jordanian bus raced ours.

Eilat had an airport and supermarket, museum and zoo, the hotels were few and a hundred or so beatniks lived by the shore in shacks they had built out of tin, cardboard and palm fronds. I saw one Chinese. A Dutch youth described himself as, 'Clean in heart and mind.' I noticed the beatniks sitting in cheap cafés with a stray puppy or kitten, feeding it omelette or chocolate milk before beginning the meal themselves.

On the beach a boy introduced himself as *Le Patron* and offered me a room for one Israeli pound a night. he had built a number of shelters and made a living by letting them. Mine, a bargain, with *tout comfort,* as he said, had sliding panel windows and a sunken drum of drinking water by the door six metres from the water's edge. *Le Patron* fished at dawn, delivered free fish to his tenants and even helped start the fire for those breakfasts, the most delicious of my life.

Business was *Le Patron's* passion. He was twenty-two, probably slightly mad and certainly highly organized, with steel-rimmed spectacles, white pointed face (he had not time for sunbathing) and a going-to-seed straw hat. Over his bathing suit he put a clean white shirt if he went to 'town', (the supermarket). *Le Patron,* when he wasn't preparing a *chambre* for a new arrival, made rocking chairs and traded turquoise from 'King Solomon's' mines. He managed to obtain some good books in English for me, 'Idiots,' he called the other beatniks. Like an old man disapproving of the younger generation, he described two beatniks who had set out in a rowing boat for an island they had seen pictured on a postcard which happened to be seven kilometres inside Egyptian territory. An Israeli patrol boat stopped them in time from crossing the frontier, he said digustedly.

An American Jewish girl asked if she might sit by me on the beach for when she was alone men bothered her. She seemed rather heavily made up for swimming and carried a small suitcase of beach equipment. 'Don't you find hashish better after the first time?' her conversation began. I was not qualified to answer. Beatniks, she said, revolted her. I told her about one who, for a bet had swum to Jordan, bought a packet of cigarettes with an American dollar in Aqaba and swum back. She was unimpressed by his luck/stupidity/danger because she hadn't really grasped the political situation. She didn't like Israelis either, 'They're *crude.*' Her mother was travelling with her. 'She hates every minute. We have never seen poor Jews before and here there are so many.'

Evenings I cooked by the lapping sea with the lights of Aqaba flickering across the bay and in the morning the sun rose over the red Arabian mountains with its first rays shining into my door. I floated, suspended in the clear water, my shadow on the sea bed and fish passing below. How far I had had to travel to arrive.

Zealots

'You have brought the English weather with you,' was the greeting when I returned to Masada for the second season. Rain had made the site a morass of mud, the mountain path too slippery to climb. A frightening roar had woken me the first morning: it was a river. Without vegetation to subdue it the water rushed over the hills, channelled by a gully, towards Herod's aqueduct (traces of which remained) that had been perfectly placed to catch the torrent. Herod's cisterns would have been full to overflowing with enough for a year or more after a few hours of such a storm.

This winter we had our own kitchens and we appreciated hot soup the staff kept ready. I found our archaeologist trying to dry his anorak over the tea urn. 'Have *you* ever seen such rain?' he asked. Familiar faces lessened the strangeness of being back, I settled down.

We spent the day photographing the desert waterfalls, a once-in-a-lifetime chance for us. The next day we did get up Masada. I saw restoration of the storerooms had been completed (though 2% of the area would remain in its original state), excavated buildings were taking shape, the plateau was circled by the now clearly defined casement wall.

In the mud, moving rocks was the only work we could do. Then rain began again and the thirty or forty volunteers had to shelter in the big cistern. We built a fire and sang and danced. It was a good morning after all.

Continuing rain made life uncomfortable and prompted a group who wanted more pocket money, better movies, richer meals, to increase their complaints. What would have become of them the first season? This year we had separate hot showers for men and women, permanent WCs, weekly movies, full time cooks . . . luxuries to me. Those who wanted to leave would be driven back to Beersheva immediately the professor announced. Some American and English volunteers did go. I admired the organizers for inviting foreigners, they could have kept the project exclusively Israeli. As it was, hundreds from other countries participated gladly.

The storm tore at our tent, every minute the rip at the top lengthened. Which would come first, total collapse or quieter weather? The Australian girl, her feet in a puddle, calmly ate an orange. Israeli soldier girls lay unmoving on their beds, an Uzi machine-gun beside the girl due for next guard duty. Fortunately my clothes were packed in plastic bags, those I wore still dry and warm. Good-natured shouts signalled the slow collapse of another tent, trapping some inside. Was it the professor inspecting the damage, only brown eyes visible from his balaclava?

The canteen tent ripped down the middle, those at the top row went next. A wind of extraordinary force battered us. A tent coming down makes an elegant bow, one knows the moment to leave. The girls cried, 'Hold it!' while I clutched my pack and wriggled out. Luckily we lost both of ours in daylight. The soldiers had another ready as soon as the old tent split.

I dreamed I heard chewing noises and awoke to find the end of my blanket reduced to grey fluff. A Dutch girl in the next bed screamed, a desert rat had given birth to six little ones in her rucksack, there being no dry place outside. After sampling my blanket it had chosen her cashmere twin-set to chew up for a softer nest. The poor girl was distraught and the professor promised to send for the pest control, meanwhile, a cat dispatched to our tent went to sleep on the Australian girl's bed.

The desert rats were reddish, with blunt noses, short tails and bright eyes; not unpleasant looking unless it was your rucksack they had occupied. I asked the Dutch girl why she had bought such good clothes for work. My question provoked another outburst. Since her convent upbringing, where she had been forced to wear a coarse shift, even while bathing so as not to see her own body, she had wanted soft beautiful clothes. Upon arrival in Israel she had fallen in love with an Israeli. They would marry as soon as her conversion had been completed, she said. As for the desert rats, an efficient pest control service removed them from our life.

* * *

The sun rose in an innocent blue sky. Immediately the hills were green. Tiny hyacinths came out. Waterfalls had left deep scars but only our rubbish, crumpled tents and muddy laundry spoiled the landscape.

Our archaeologist saved the storeroom in which I had been working the year before. 'So you will feel at home.' Teams were larger this season, we finished the huge room in record time. It was a dull one and must have originally contained vital goods that had been used in antiquity or taken away without leaving a trace. The Australian girl found the only coin.

Instead of the usual contingent of soldiers or parachutists during two cycles (of two weeks each) Israelis from the submarines helped dig. The boy who joined our team was the best worker I had ever met: thoughtfulness, willingness, strength, combined with intelligence were rare, or if people had these qualities, as he had, they reserved them for other occupations.

Another member of our team, a well-meaning American college boy who had never seen a wheelbarrow replied, 'Sure!' when asked if he could push one. He insisted we fill it up, then ran faster and faster, wobbling down the ramp to dump the earth and stones over the precipice. Just in time someone yelled to him, 'Let go!' as the loaded wheelbarrow crashed the barrier and flew over the edge.

The annual ceremony of tree planting in Israel is one to which tourists contribute. We put in a few little pomegranate trees by the water tap and hoped they would grow. Herod's Garrison, and the Zealots and in the 5th century, Byzantine monks living there briefly, cultivated kitchen gardens on Masada.

A motherly Jerusalem housewife-volunteer in our team commented on how easy planting was. 'Easy?' I was puzzled. She described the hills around her house, rocky and bare,

127

when she had first come to Israel. Her job had been to carry up buckets of earth, 'without donkey', before trees could be put there. Her early days in Israel, she told me, were , 'So wonderful, so simple, such good relationships between peoples.' She had come from Russia as a sportswoman with the Olympics. 'No, no, I no sportswoman. My friends make me certificate so I get here. Live with my uncle in Tel Aviv, very poor man. They buy one bread. I say, no thank you, not hungry. After, he find me a job in laundry. I very ashamed. I cry and cry. I never work before I come here. In the laundry no machines. Scrub, scrub. The first day they say, where your sandwich? I no bring. A girl give me half hers. It is cucumber. The next day my arms, so. Like this. Can't move. After, after, all right. I learn. I *want* to come to Israel. Now I help new immigrants from Russia. Russian accent perfect they say, "Like yesterday." '

I saw an archaeologist discover a scroll fragment, the most precious of finds. The brown piece, with its barely discernible letters, he could read and knew from where in the Bible the few words came. He carried it cautiously in a cardboard box, his expression radiant. A famous novelist who visited Masada found a bit of a 'scroll' beside the path. The tourist's excitement was extinguished, however, when it was revealed to be a warped piece of shoe sole (modern).

Ben Gurion was coming to Masada and markers for his helicopter were laid out on clear ground near the stores. Flares went off. Very soon he was with us. His direct manner put me at ease. 'Why did you come to Israel?' His friendly eyes settled on my face.

'It was an accident,' I said, meaning I had no reason as Jews had.

'A good accident,' the professor kindly interposed. Ben Gurion, after hearing how I was enjoying my visit, told me of his fondness for London.

To his wife's parting remark, 'You will soon find a husband here,' the word *'shalom'*, peace, was all I said. It is a beautiful greeting or parting salutation and it is also the perfect word for occasions such as this on which one can think of nothing else. The professor led the Ben Gurions off towards the newly discovered bath-house and the rest of our afternoon, after such an encounter, was totally empty.

Outside the main office a case exhibited important and daily finds. Although padlocked, the horde of silver shekels and half-shekels discovered beneath a Zealot's floor was so rare that a soldier guarded it. So handsome was the soldier, girls went along to see both.

Eleven *ostricans* were found, little pieces each with one of the eleven names whom the professor concluded were those Zealots who drew lots to kill one another after putting to death the others on that last evening, an event described in detail by Josephus. I watched the professor; he stood where they had been unearthed, transfixed. The same handwriting was on all the pieces. On one shard, beautifully and clearly written, was the name of the Zealot commander, Eleazar ben Yair. The sight of the present commander holding the lot drawn by the last commander would answer those who would ask me, 'And what was, in your experience, the most dramatic moment of the dig?'

As a treat, after finishing another storeroom, we began work in the Herodian administrative rooms next door. There we could dig with a small team, at a calm pace, in a room with door and window; a home rather than a public building. Red and white frescoes, bright when found there, faded quickly and despite treatment from a specialist, many flaked off. Arrow heads, silver plated armour scales and, in pieces, an elaborate Roman lamp were more encouraging finds than the few broken jars in the last storeroom. The professor glanced in. 'You're sweating!' Yes, but we were enjoying ourselves! We went on into the next little room, left as it had been by the Zealots with two column sections that served them as tables, (clear on both stones was the Jewish mason's mark). In the corner, hiding part of a Herodian fresco, a bath had been built, its stopper was still in place. Such homely details touched me. The long store rooms stretching uneventfully before us during weeks of hard work, weren't comparable. If I complained about anything, even the weather, our archaeologist was liable to say, with a twinkle in his eye, 'I think you are not happy here. I think you want to go back to the storerooms.' Once he came to find our room empty. 'Why aren't you working?' We had gone to the edge of the cliff to stare up at the marvellous cloud of migrating storks drifting on air currents above Masada. I asked, 'Isn't this a special

129

occasion for stopping work?' He looked up.

'Yes, it's a special occasion.'

The first resistance fighter against the British in Palestine came to Masada for two weeks. Dead or alive, the price on his head had been high. 'What they call a modern Zealot, a man whose belief in what he does is absolute,' our archaeologist described this man. 'Gradually others joined him to build Israel. His job now is head-keeper to Ben Gurion.'

'Bodyguard?'

'Yes.' I wanted to talk to him but there was no opportunity.

While we were listening to the news of the Russian cosmonaut on the transistor, an American diplomat, digging with us, found a coin. 'Isn't that great!' the American cried.

'Yes,' I replied, then noticing he was referring to his coin, I went over and admired it. My first miserable little coin had been of the same type.

With 400 in camp and the excavation nearly over, we were under pressure to finish and tidy our areas. No bodies of the defenders had been discovered except a family of three, probably the commander, his wife and child, hidden under burned material in the northern palace, and some bodies of those who may have died and been buried during the siege. On the last day we found a Roman sword.

* * *

For two following winters I came again to Israel to see more of the country. The kibbutz on which I first volunteered to work and which accepted me, consisted of many small houses among pine and eucalyptus trees beside the Mediterranean. I was given my own one-room house with a balcony and garden. Each visitor was lent an electric water heater, a paraffin stove, boots and blue working clothes. We were expected to work an eight hour day, had ten lira a week pocket money and were allowed five free days a month for travelling around the country. This kibbutz was a pleasant site with about 500 members. Laundry, postage, medical care were free, as were films, concerts and use of the kibbutz library. Food was heathful and plentiful, though it could be monotonous. Israelis had their own houses with kitchens where they could prepare what they wanted when they liked, while we volunteers ate at fixed hours in the main dining room with the majority of kibbutz-nicks.

I started as a lemon-picker. The large thorny trees surprised me. The first morning a fine rain began and everyone ran. 'What's happening?' I shouted, running after them.

'It's raining,' they cried, taking shelter in a shed.

The next week I picked oranges from heavily-laden trees in grassy groves called 'Paradice', or Paradise. Each worker had three boxes a day to fill which contained about 600 kilo of oranges. The stem must be cut close to the fruit thus leaving no sharp bit to scratch the others, neither must the stem base be pulled out as this would leave the orange liable to decay. I worked steadily to finish my quota, resisting the temptation to eat them until afterwards. Grapefruit were even better; nothing was as good as grapefruit off the trees. I kept a thirty kilo bag in my room for snacks.

The 6-8 year-olds visited us in the paradice. They were the healthiest looking, most self-possessed children I had ever met. The whole traffic-free kibbutz was theirs in which to play, bicycles, donkey carts, doll houses and swings were theirs for the taking. Parents kept their very young children at home after work and on Shabat, otherwise babies were cared for in the nursery. I thought the kibbutz ideal for the young and the old, both were well looked after and never lonely. At my age, I needed a challenge. A man with a concentration camp number tattooed on his wrist told me, 'When I came to Israel, I was dust.' For him the whole kibbutz was paradise.

From Berkshire they had imported bees. 'Have you come to see *our* queen?' they asked me. I heard about the carp but as working in the fish ponds was 'man's work', I never went there. Next I pruned fruit trees. Top branches killed by the wind had to be cut out correctly and a job that required a little skill or thought increased my enjoyment of it. They changed me to work I considered significant. We put cactus-like plants in the sand which took root immediately and soon grew, spreading all over the surface, gradually altering the soil so that eventually trees and crops might be planted. In this way a small, sandy, vine-growing community became a large, fertile, shady farm.

During a storm we painted army gun rests in the carpentry shop. Another of the kibbutz businesses was the dairy and I could hear the cows' low moos from my house, milked night *and* day, I was told. 'If they are used to the demand, they produce.'

'I suppose your chickens lay two eggs a day?'

'We're coming to that!' The cows, given orange peel waste from the orange juice factory, rolled their eyes and tossed their heads with real fury knowing they had to eat this before getting anything better.

On cloudy Shabats I loved walking along the beach. Ancient pottery and coins were revealed by rain or high seas washing away a layer of top soil. Traces of the Roman town that had once covered the area were everywhere; alfalfa had been planted in the former Roman hippodrome and white flowering bushes grew where the outlines of Roman gardens were still clear. Marble columns lay in the grass. I found two big Byzantine coins to clink together in my pocket. I came across a ruined little Roman bath-house in the sand and recognized the caldarium right away.

Kibbutz members cooked each volunteer a cake for Shabat and I returned to find mine in my room. The porcupine that always upset my dustbin had left some quills behind. Brahms, one of the many cats named after composers, gazed over the edge of the roof. For here and now, this was my home.

'Woman's work' was in the kitchens. I suspected any 'man's work' would be more interesting and applied for it. One of the 'easiest' jobs, sowing, I couldn't manage at all. With a sack of grain slung around one's shoulder, one took a handful, a certain sized step and scattered the grain the right distance. It was Biblical and the idea appealed to me but I fell over my feet, threw the stuff the wrong way, a whole fistful at once and was told I wasn't on a straight course for more than two paces. They didn't know what to do with me for the rest of the morning so I slunk off and weeded.

For bananas, a job described as 'difficult', we were transported to a leafy jungle where a man with a machette led two or three of us to developed, but still green, bunches. One of the followers positioned himself with the bananas resting on his shoulder: the trick was to start forward as the machette man cut the bunch from the branch and not to drop it on its sudden release. Carrying awkward bunches weighing 40 kilo, over rough ground to the truck just demanded concentration. If dropped, they were damaged, unsaleable and abandoned. I could not bear to see these mounds of wasted fruit ripening to perfection and kept staggering home with them. I ate bananas until I should have turned yellow. The fruit grew under protective plastic covers, ripped off by the machette man, often to the shock of rats who were living within. I saw rats leap off others' backs when the bananas were cut down, never knowing if they had been in my own bunches.

Chickens were supposed to be quieter when caught and loaded for market at midnight. They weren't. We pulled the birds from their cages by one leg, four in either hand, and rushed them squawking, pecking, and feathers flying to the waiting lorry. When they had all gone we ate huge omelettes and halva, a very sweet sweet. Night work meant a free morning for swimming and only two hours washing-up at dinner. Washing-up was done behind a counter which everyone passed entering or leaving the dining room so it was a sociable job I would have liked if I hadn't preferred above all to be outdoors.

An English family who planned to go to Masada the following week asked if I would like to be their guide. Of course I agreed though to earn the extra day off from the kibbutz, to which I was not yet entitled, I applied for work on Shabat. I was allocated potato peeling. An old Israeli working with me had not heard the latest news so I told him, thinking he would be pleased. Two Syrian fighters had just been shot down. All he said was, 'If you are glad of someone else's disaster, the same thing might happen to you. Let us be grateful no one shot down one of ours.' Since then it is surprising how often I have had the occasion to remember his words.

I met the English family whom I would accompany, at the King David hotel in Jerusalem. We drove to Arad, then over the hills where the Dead Sea came into view. Masada, approached from the back, so as to say, wasn't dramatic because one came to it from higher ground. Only when standing at the foot of the Roman ramp were they impressed. Already I had asked the woman's two children, 'What news from England?'

'The Beatles have grown moustaches!' they replied in unison. Now the family began to question me on the facts of the 10th Legion's siege. We discussed the choice of suicide rather than slavery. One of the children asked why Moses had remained in the wilderness for forty years and our driver volunteered a reason.

'Moses knew slaves did not make good pioneers. He wanted to wait for their children's generation of free men to settle Israel.'

The English woman heard the bird call, a 'whee, whee' that was almost a whining. 'What's that?' I pointed to birds resembling starlings.

'The orange under their wings shows only when they fly. They are called Tristan's Grackle and are quite rare.' I went on to tell them about a man the BBC sent out to record the birds. First he visited the site and was invited to dig. We were working in ash, rich with small finds such as hairpins and broken lamps dumped there by the Romans from the bath-house, for after the Zealots' mass suicide, the Romans had cleared out the few buildings they wanted to use for themselves.

The BBC man became absorbed in the work, he muttered whenever I passed, 'I've got to go and record those damn birds . . . .' I assured him they were always around our dustbins in the morning, the birds could be recorded easily, so he spent the day with us as a sifter.

'Yes!' cried the girls seeing the orange-backed wings as the birds reluctantly took flight. We started to climb. I showed them wood in the ramp, carried by slaves from the oasis of En Gedi, which looked fresh even after nineteen hundred years. They were as interested as I. On Masada the mother picked up rusty sardine tins, the children quite independently collected paper and orange peel (thoughtlessly dropped by other visitors) and put the garbage in the bins provided.

The Romans may have kept horses in the little synagogue, the earliest ever found. I showed them where the Zealots had added to and restored this most important building. There had been a possibility that the thick-walled bath-house had another use until we turned over the first soot-backed tile revealing the caldarium's heating system. I showed them a primitive duck scratched on a wall and over a bench, where guards, dreaming of a fresher landscape, had drawn a boat, and palms. Some of the Zealot ovens remained. I even pointed out the monk's chair and one of the children rested in it. There were stones the size of grapefruit rounded by the Zealots as missiles that lay unused. Every building had its story, every discovery, another.

In Herod's northern palace the younger girl observed, 'It's so cool here!'

'It is one of the reasons Herod chose this spot,' I said. She leaned over the abyss where fresh air rushed up from the deep ravine.

'I wish I could spit out my plates,' she murmured longingly, her red hair waving in the breeze. The rock above shaded only this place on Masada.

The other child asked, 'Is that a hamster?' A furry animal looked out from a crevice.

'They are desert rats, as tame as hamsters,' I smiled to see they had survived the pest controller's efforts.

On our way back to Jerusalem, we went via the Dead Sea and the children expected the water there to look like syrup because I said walking in it one had the feeling of wearing wellington boots several sizes too large. I announced, 'There is no life here,' and that moment we saw tiny swimming creatures in puddles a couple of metres from the water's edge. We could think of no explanation.

'How extraordinary,' the English woman said, 'we must write a letter to *The Times.*'

Along an especially lonely part of the road we met an Israeli lorry out of petrol. Our driver was going to syphon off some of ours but before he could, his VIP passenger had knelt in the road to help the lorry driver with the messy job. This titled English woman who was not Jewish wanted to show somehow, I think, friendliness to a people she liked and admired. 'She is a *real* lady,' the driver told me at the end of that long day. 'I've done this trip many times and never have enjoyed it so much.'

Our archaeologist, who lived in Jerusalem, would let me

135

stay in his spare room for the night. He was munching chocolate and sitting wrapped in an electric blanket when I arrived. 'How I long for summer,' he declared. Jerusalem's altitude kept the city comparatively cool in summer and often cold during the winter, while my kibbutz farther south, by the sea, remained a moderate temperature. Several English postcards lay among the dictionaries on his desk where he had been working. The lavatory, papered with London maps prompted me to ask how he liked my city. 'I love London,' he used his tender tone of voice which I remembered so well from the discovery of my first coin.

* * *

From the bus I surveyed kibbutz banana and orange groves, automatically comparing their quality with ours. The first sight of my kibbutz, its little houses, sand dunes, the few Brahman cattle under a mimosa tree by the bus stop was endearing. Like a gargoyle, a giant lizard posed on my roof. I took sandwiches to the beach. A mare and her foal galloped in the sea. Furniture painting would be my afternoon's work.

* * *

Every spring I automatically went back to work in London, my money ran out, my migratory habit had become a routine. As usual the ship from Haifa to Marseilles stopped in Naples for a couple of hours and though it was raining hard I went ashore just because I always did. Near a quay a big swastika had been chalked on the wall. I thought, I'll rub it out on the way back to the ship, changed my mind, and started on it then. The rough surface of the wall made the job difficult. I did not notice a man watching until I finished and looked up. 'Thank you,' he said. A star of David was stitched on his jacket. He walked away and the swfulness of anti-Semitism hit me, the suffering it caused overcame me. I didn't want to think about it, what was it to do with me? Why couldn't I forget? I walked in the rain with my head back so the tears would be washed off, so my face would be washed clean by the rain.

I found the man who had thanked me was also a passenger. During the voyage he came and sat by me on deck sometimes, covering himself completely with a blanket if the sea was rough. I learned his name was Aaron and that he was going to England to study. It was his first trip abroad. He was from Tel Aviv.

*　*　*

I missed the night ferry to London and near the Paris station walked around looking for a hotel. Seventeen hotels at which I asked for a room were full, at the eighteenth the owner offered me the sofa in the sitting room, all he had, there would be no charge. Grateful and exhausted, I thanked him. In the dimly lit hall I noticed a vase of carnations and started coughing and sneezing with my usual hay fever symptoms. The owner brought blankets and turned up the light to make my 'bed'. 'They're plastic!' I wailed, seeing the flowers clearly.

'Yes, I'm afraid so.' He noticed my tan, 'Where did you get so brown?'

'Israel.'

'I'm a Jew. I have been to Israel. How did *you* like it?'

'Very much,' I wasn't going to be able to forget anything. The date was 1st May 1967.

30th May. I thought war would come at any moment. Ten thousand joined the 'Solidarity with Israel' march in Hyde Park. Aaron, here to study English, visited me only to say he had volunteered and was on his way to the airport and back to Israel.

Sir Francis Chichester's lone voyage around the world earned first place in the TV news. 'They should use *him* to test the blockade of the Straits of Tiran.' Everyone agreed.

Next followed scenes of shelters and blood-donors in Tel Aviv.

2nd June. The television news showed Arab mobs screaming for the destruction of Israel. 'Oh, I *will* miss those Jaffa grapefruit!' my landlady expressed heart-felt concern.

A girl in our flat looked at me, 'Why are *you* worried?

137

You're not a Jew are you?'

'If the Israelis win, they will be anxious to make peace as soon as possible. If the Arabs win, it may be hard to stop the slaughter,' I explained.

'You exaggerate, I'm sure,' she cooed.

A friend, 'Don't tell her I told you, but after my mother gave all the money she could for Israel, she gave her new mink coat.'

4th June. Wake up weeping. I think it is a horrible nightmare. It is worse waking and knowing it isn't.

5th June. Very early I telephoned a friend. He asked, 'Haven't you heard? Fighting has begun. Israeli tanks are advancing.'

'Advancing?'

'Yes.'

Israel claimed to have destroyed hundreds of enemy planes. 'Bloody fighting in Syria.' Who was lost? Who was wounded? 'Jews pray at the Wailing Wall.' The French news reported Israelis swimming in the Suez Canal. Gradually the papers print the whole story.

A letter from Jerusalem listed names of those I knew, some are wounded, all are alive. Another from an archaeologist's wife, 'One has something to live for and something to fight for in a life worth living.'

A girl who came to tea talked brightly about, 'The rights of the Palestinians.' She thought, 'The Israelis should *go*. I don't know where exactly . . . .' She had not met a person of either nationality and when I expressed desire that both have a home she declared herself, 'More interested in wild life preservation.'

Aaron returned, wearing his old jeans, carrying a battered suitcase, he looked worn out. Trying to cheer him, I asked, 'How was it, *winning?*' He couldn't speak, many of his friends had been killed in Syria. He sat down, he had nowhere to go. I made coffee and sandwiches. 'Ask the rabbi for help,' I advised. Aaron refused, he did not know how to pray, neither had he ever been to synagogue. 'You can sleep here.' I put a mattress on the floor.

'OK,' he said.

A letter from Jerusalem described our archaeologist's 'glowing face', now that he could visit, for the first time, the caves in Qurmaran, where the Dead Sea Scrolls were found.

Jerusalem

The storm began the night our Turkish ship left Naples. Having to hold on to the side of my bunk all night just to stay in it made sleep impossible. As soon as there was light enough I climbed to the top deck and took refuge in a cubby-hole by the swimming pool. Here, sufficiently protected, I felt better in the fresh air. Wind marbled the sea with froth, a mountainous horizon of waves reared towards us like monsters, lightning cracked; truly heaven in a rage. Chairs shooting back and forth across the deck were reduced to sticks. The pool emptied at a tilt of the ship, at another refilled with a roar.

Two other passengers who managed to reach the top deck, also decided to stay there. One of them, a new emigrant going to Israel, had won a lot of blankets in a bingo game, and by sharing them, greatly added to our comfort. He exclaimed at the most violent lurches of the ship, 'How we must suffer to get to Israel!' The other, a French-speaking Israeli, told us he had been less afraid during the Six Day War when he had simply been shot in the leg during the first half hour of fighting.

Though it seemed impossible, the storm worsened. For two days the kitchens ceased to function and meals consisted of an apple and a hunk of bread and cheese for those who could collect the food. The crew gnawed theirs sitting cross-legged on the floor, officers ate in their cabins and we ate on the top deck. I had some dried fruit, bread and sardines, and a little stove, so we had snacks and coffee. We were now four; an exhausted bird had joined us.

Most of the time we dozed but the second night I was woken by silence. The engines had stopped. In vain I tried to turn on the swimming pool lights, then, cautiously crossing the deck, felt my way below. The only sign of life my torch revealed was cockroaches running across the walls. On a ship silence and darkness are alarming.

We were relieved by the arrival of dawn, then we noticed Crete looming in the distance. The new emigrant went to find life jackets. It was curious we were not already wearing them, up to that time we hadn't considered disaster inevitable. With the jackets, he brought the news that an anchor had been lost. We could hear the radio-operator repeating his useless message, S.O.S., S.O.S., S.O.S., the nearest ship couldn't reach us for hours.

Uneasiness led me to explore. Why were our engines silent? The first breath of the sickly, muggy atmosphere below convinced me our refuge was the better place. For their own safety, the captain had ordered passengers (we were recognized as exceptions), to remain in the salon. I saw those who had not a stable hold, skidding over the shiny floor. Surprisingly, only one had a bandaged head, and three, broken arms. Out on deck, if we let go for a careless moment, we could be washed overboard.

I braced myself against the walls of lurching corridors, I climbed down every ladder as far as I could go. More frightening than their stopping was the suddenness of the engine's starting, the throbbing, pounding filled my head with noise. An elated engineer rushed forward and hugged me with joy. He had started them! After the worry and shock, I gradually felt relief. Sweaty, greasy, smiling, he banged on doors, and no matter how bruised or sick, everyone reappeared to share the good news. Our break-down had been caused, the engineer reported, by someone's giving us the *Evil Eye*, a matter to which *he* had attended. The captain went around wishing us, 'Happy trip!' and forgotten, the storm decreased. How had this shipping line been dvertised? 'Fun, Relaxation, Comfort and Luxury,' I think. Without a single one of these attractions we had enjoyed it. Nothing makes you feel better than surviving.

* * *

Naan was the station in Israel where we waited for the train to come in on the single track. We waited a long time, and when it did come the steps were coated with ice. The armed guard changed into our train and laughing, called out, 'There's snow in Jerusalem!' Then we began the climb between the hills. Soon the ground was white, and a couple held their child to the window for her first sight of snow. The wire fence following the track on one side which, before the Six Day War, had divided Israel from Jordan, was cut.

Like the child with her snow, I couldn't help an 'Oh!'

Under deep snow Jerusalem resembled a European resort except that the mixture of tourists, kibbutznicks, Arabs, Orthodox Jews and monks pouring from the station would be unlikely in any other capital. I made my way through deep slush and was sorry to see the pavements further blocked by trees broken by the weight of snow. As no buses were operating I walked to the nearest hospice. The nun who answered my knock, stood tutting her tongue, listening to my story. She let me in and from then on referred to me as, 'Pauvre chèrie.' The snowstorm had wrecked their lights, heat and water supply, so the nun gave me candles, extra blankets and a bucket of water that clanked with broken ice as I carried it to my room.

Before unpacking I had to go to the Old City, I had to see all Jerusalem to comprehend that barriers, no-man's land and opposing soldiers no longer divided it. In the past, at Notre Dame the road had ended at a blank wall crowned with barbed wire. Now a wide clear road swept down to Jaffa Gate altering the scene so utterly that while I walked, I questioned my memory of the past.

During Jordanian rule what remained of the Temple Areas Western Wall, the most holy place for Jews, had been built over and the only exposed section confined to a back alley. I had photographed Arab children playing hopscotch there on my first visit years ago. This time I found my way instinctively through the narrow streets leading to an enormous portion of the Wall now cleared of Arab houses. The massiveness of the Wall building blocks, the perfection of the joins were typical Herodian construction. On that dark, cold, wet afternoon, the ground still piled with rubble, only two men were there. Being alone on my trips I studied things with the care I might otherwise have given to a companion. In front of this Wall past and present seemed equally poignant; it was a place where one would want to pray.

On the way back, in David Street a familiar figure in an anorak, head down, camera around his neck, came towards me. I recognized my Masada archaeologist. After he had recovered from the shock of meeting me he echoed my thoughts by saying, 'I'm living in one of the most beautiful cities in the world. All the time I want to go and walk and look. The victory was one of the most amazing of all wars but what have we won? The world begins to hate us for it. Again we are alone as we always have been. We are on an island of democracy in the Middle East but to the Americans and the Russians we are merely a pawn. So many boys have died just so we can live a little longer. Why can't they give us peace!' We walked through the snowy deserted streets until our ways parted. 'Ring me tomorrow and I will tell you if there is an archaeological job for you,' he said, 'Shalom.'

Flickering candles had been placed on the stairs of the dark hospice. An Irish priest lit one for my room. His parents' cottage in Ireland had been lit by candles, he told me, and he, the youngest of a large family, felt strange at the idea of returning. 'I've lived here so many years *this* seems like home. Those trees you see broken under the snow, I planted those with my own hands. In the Mandate days there used to be Irish soldiers who patrolled outside . . . .' The priest smiled at the memory, he looked back to that day as I would look back to this one.

The work available was with a survey team consisting of an archaeologist, two archaeological students and a volunteer called Steve who had come to Israel at the start of the Six Day War. Our Masada archaeologist offered to put me up in more comfortable surroundings but the hospice was central, the survey team could easily fetch me at 5 a.m. every day of the two weeks I was to help them.

Our job was to collect pottery shards lying on the surface. We drove from site to site where ancient towns or villages once existed and recorded the types of pottery found at each. Our survey-area, south of Hebron, a military area, necessitated soldiers accompanying us. An armed soldier remained with the jeep, one joined us, adding a shard now and again to the collection. Their presence could be comforting. Road-widening work in the vicinity had been given to Arab refugees who stared after us with the look of an enemy, such as I had not experienced, a look that seemed to say, 'Your life is worth nothing.'

'The Arab refugees hate us but we must give them work,' one of the students guessed what I was thinking. 'The only hope is with their children. Perhaps for them we will not be monsters.'

Among the Bedouin Arabs the situation was completely different: we were the *guests* of these desert tribesmen. Often the Bedouin, camping on the ancient sites we investigated, served tea which was excellent after our cold drive.

At the first stop we each walked in a different direction looking for pottery rims and bases from which dates could be established. Steve's favourite period was between 4000-3000 BCE. He hunted its evidence intently, always being last back to the jeep. Surface finds were compared with old records, visible traces of buildings or installations were noted. The students drew and photographed unusual tombs. So many sites existed within our limited area that I lost count. This survey provided me with a chance to see part of the country that I wouldn't have otherwise, my only regret each day was being told to stop work. Not far from Crusader ruins we came to a Byzantine graveyard, recently robbed, and looking pitiful with its narrow graves cut in bed-rock, empty except for rain water, not a shard remained.

Hebron, where we picked up our guards, was cold, ridges of snow remained on the hills. Farther south our fingers and toes unfroze, the landscape became more familiar to me from Masada days. 'We Israelis love the Negev, here we find peace and God,' the archaeologist said. Four thousand young pines had been planted by a forestation project. I remembered the Argentinian I had met on his way to Israel who had promised to, 'Make the desert live again.'

The track was the patrol-road along the former Jordanian frontier, and Steve delightedly informed me, 'Infiltrators often lay mines along this road!'

'Don't tell me now!' I cried. Getting reactions pleased Steve. He was plodding and well-meaning, people underestimated him. TEA was what we were really thinking about. In this village mud-brick houses replaced the black tents because the Israeli government was trying to persuade the nomads to settle, to grow crops, pay taxes, and send their children to school. Whatever their living conditions, the Bedouins' hospitality is generous. Steve appreciatively sipped the tea which was brought to us. 'We will have to do a *Michelin Guide* to Arab villages. This is certainly three star tea . . . .' We ate our picnic lunch, leaving useful empty tins and some grapefruit, for the Arabs. Steve wouldn't hand over his baked bean tin. 'It would be an insult, it's *filthy*.' He was terribly anxious to improve relations between Arab and Jew in any way possible.

One of the students, the worst of drivers, might start the morning at the wheel. Before long we would get stuck and he would raise his hands in surrender at our laughter. 'You couldn't even drive a bloody train,' Steve declared. Looking at a tomb rather than the road, the student drove into a wall. Then at full speed, tooting, he overtook a camel as one of the car doors fell off. Even the Arab on the camel laughed. The archaeologist was the best driver. It was a point of honour with him to make the jeep take him where he wanted to go, whether over rocks, up mountain goat-tracks or across desert. We jumped ditches that would have stopped anyone else.

A guest, an American archaeologist, for some reason rigged out with Arab headdress and three cameras, joined us one day. 'You'd better hold on,' I advised, trying to be friendly.

'Oh, I know all about jeep travel,' he answered, 'I've just been to See-neigh,' (as he pronounced it). We hit a bump that almost tossed him out. 'One doesn't expect rough spots on *this* road,' he muttered indignantly. Realizing there wasn't a spare tool for him to poke about with he suggested, 'Well, I'll use yours.' I decided to be first out and away when we halted. 'You don't say,' he would repeat after every comment we made. He photographed a flock of sheep. The shepherd, believing the American must be a sheik in such an outfit, saluted him. The American gaped back, open-mouthed.

To avoid our guest I worked on the far side of the hill. Extremely ferocious local village dogs often attacked us. We would wait for one to come near and then by hitting it with a single stone frighten away the pack. This once, when the dogs came barking after me, there were no stones within reach, no villagers in sight to call them off. Recognizing my helplessness, the dogs circled with hysterical fury. Would the animals attack if I stood still and ignored them? Their snarling, their snapping teeth and maddened eyes, made me decide it was too late for the test. I was frightened, and between grabbing handfuls of earth to throw in their faces, I tried to make an orderly retreat. Perfectly timed, our soldier came over the hill to find me. The dogs fled when he raised his rifle. He laughed at my look of gratitude. Being a Jewish refugee from North Africa meant he could speak to me in French. The soldier's usual job was interrogating suspected terrorists because of course, he also spoke perfect Arabic. I asked if he had to hit prisoners for information. 'No,' he answered. 'We give them a cigarette and tea. They are relieved. They talk.' The soldier smoked a great deal. When I commented on this he explained. 'Nerves of the job. I am often alone among many Arabs. Perhaps there will be trouble. What can I do? I smoke.' I was glad he had not known how frightened I had been just by a pack of dogs.

Our last day's task was to organize the cleaning of a third century synagogue. Stones from the synagogue had been reused in buildings throughout the town and what remained *in situ* lay buried beneath rubbish. While we waited for workmen to help us, Arab children surrounded the jeep. A little boy detached himself from the others and announced in English, 'Majestic King Hussein is a very nice man.' The Israeli student heard.

He asked, smiling, 'And what about Prince Dyan?' The child made a face as though he had tasted something bad, then overcome by the situation, hid behind the car.

* * *

Occasionally I spent Saturday with an American couple who had volunteered to work a year in Israel. A holiday of theirs in London they described enthusiastically for my benefit, and joked about being arrested. 'The police were real polite except this Irish guy who caught us speeding. He said, "You're *Jews.*" like we were *born* criminals.' Their stories were interrupted by their rushing to the stove to check the meal's progress, or in letting in, and throwing out, an un-house-trained kitten. Afterwards we walked to the Western Wall, following the Orthodox Jews in their formal costume and fur-brimmed hats. 'Awful,' my friend complained. 'No wonder we are hated if people think we are all like that: freaks from the past, closed in religion.' The young man bitterly criticized their, 'narrow-mindedness.' His girlfriend interposed, 'I went to the Wailing Wall just after the war. Sure, I was moved. I wept. I felt something. A bit later I came back. All these guys in big black hats and side curls tell me I have to go to a certain part to pray. They *commercialize* it.'

'If your feelings are sincere why should superficialities touch you?' I asked.

She looked at me, 'I guess you're tolerant of Jews like I'm tolerant of Christians.' I smiled; she always had the last word.

Around the corner on the southern side of the wall, they showed me the trenches of a new excavation. We returned to the western side, called the Western Wall or Wailing Wall, where people were praying, men at one section, women at another. An old woman wept loudly against the stones. 'How sad she cannot be comforted,' I observed.

The girl replied, 'The Wall *is* her comfort.'

That evening's news reported Orthodox Jews, who disapproved of work being done on Shabat, stoning the electricians who were trying to repair a cable at the hospital in central Jerusalem. 'The electricians could have been electrocuted and the hospital without lights for all *they* care! Terrible! Now do you understand our problem?' the young American demanded.

In the night, firing took place across the Jordan. I went to bed early and did not hear the planes reconnoitring. A few extra police might have been patrolling East Jerusalem the next day, otherwise the atmosphere was as usual. In the Middle East there is an underlying current of violence while calm and charm flow on the surface. To look at the church towers and dark green trees against the creamy stone walls you would not guess what ferment the Old City held.

I took Steve some herbs I bought in the souk. They were what he wanted; with them he made scented tea, the quality rating three stars like that the Bedouin had given us on our survey. Then we went to the Rockefeller museum which, after my experience of digging, I enjoyed much more than on my first visit, before it. Our Israeli guide talked about the war, 'A lot of fighting took place here as you can see. Much glass was broken but there was no looting. Unsually the first troops are not the kind who steal and besides, they are too tired. By the third day we archaeologists were here clearing up.' The office had bullet-holes in the walls, and scrawled in red, 'Israel – Arab. *Peace.*' 'I don't know who wrote it but we are going to leave it there,' he remarked. Signs, I saw in the museum's galleries, were the original ones, in English, Arabic and Hebrew. During Jordanian rule the Hebrew plaques had been covered by brown sticky paper, traces of which still showed at the edges. There were cases and cases of Steve's favourite type of pottery.

He urged me, 'Come and look!'

We got a lift home with an Israeli friend. Although we had only half-an-hour's walk I was glad to be driven and out of the wind. We passed two youths who waved, wanting a lift. The driver slowed down and then seeing that they were Arabs, he sped on again just as the boys had started to run towards us. Steve's fury caught us unawares, 'That's the most horrible thing! After all, they're human beings. In this perishing wind . . . . One day we've all got to live together.'

Our friend said quietly, 'I've reason to hate them.' We knew the Israeli's brother had been killed by Arabs.

Steve, a London East End Jew, retorted, 'You've just made two enemies who might have been friends.' Steve insisted he and I get out and walk the rest of the way home.

An English family connected with the church invited me to dinner, not because they liked me, out of boredom and longing for a new face. Where they lived, until the Six Day War, had been the Jerusalem of Jordan. 'Life in these past years has been very comfortable, as it was at the time of the British Raj. People were very nice to one,' the man began. 'Life, as I said, was easy. Now, I'm afraid all that has gone forever. I *do* believe it's best to have Jerusalem united . . . under one government or another. The trouble is, the Israelis are their own worst enemies. They can't take criticism. If you are not "for" them, you're "against" them.'

The man's wife murmured, 'Poor things, such terrible

persecution and all that . . . .'

He continued, 'I suppose you *could* call us pro-Arab. That doesn't mean we are anti-Israeli. I might say I'm anti-Zionist. Zionists are different from *Jews* . . . .'

The wife added, 'They're so quick to misinterpret what we say . . . .'

The husband explained, 'After all, we did suffer too. The children's dog was killed by shrapnel, the front gate smashed, and the garden absolutely *ruined*. How would you feel towards those who had destroyed your property?' He sat back taking a puff or two from his pipe. 'Oh, I'm not saying the Arabs didn't deserve what they got. They are cowards. What they were shouting in the street before the war was disgusting. When it came to it, they hid behind their wives or under their beds. I don't care for Jews but at least they took away their dead. The Arabs ran so fast there was no one left to do anything. The Jews did bring bread and milk to people without. Oh yes, the Jews *fight* well.' A deafening explosion followed this tirade. Shattered window glass clattered on the floor. A terrorist's house 200 metres away had been blown up as a reprisal, by Israelis.

An Arab who lived next door to the English couple called out, 'It's the Jews again,' with sophisticated resignation. 'Blowing up the houses of terrorists is a law introduced by the British in mandate days.' I mentioned this fact which placated no one.

No sooner had the survey finished than I heard of another archaeological job. Professor B., in charge of the Southern Wall excavation, was accepting volunteers. I arrived early one morning to make a good impression and hoped to be accepted even though I was a woman. 'You come to work?' a dark young man asked, and before I could look at the site, put me at the bottom of a trench to fill buckets. The workers, a gang of Jewish refugees from North Africa with Biblical names, complained if the buckets they had to lift up the ladders were too full. They would press a sweet into my hand, or ask me if I liked poetry; each had his own charming way of delaying work.

Professor B. Mazar arrived with a group of tourists to whom he explained the excavation. Later he took around group after group, responding enthusiastically to the same questions, asked again and again. He had white hair, a wide smile, and always time to give us an encouraging word.

From seven until three we worked and, being out of condition, I was hotter and more tired that first day than on any other. I learned what a luxury it was to be really hungry and eat, to be really dirty and wash, and really tired and sleep; not what my London friends would call, 'Living'.

The operation grew with more volunteers, more workers and a bulldozer to remove the top soil. An owl that lived in a niche in the wall screeched at us for the daily disturbance. It was he who was finally driven away, I'm sorry to say. One house remained against the wall, in the area of the excavation. The owner sat watching the bulldozer approach, head in hands. The Arab's little garden was slowly destroyed, and then the single tree went down. 'Even for the tree, he's getting paid double,' an archaeologist assured me. If it is a motorway, a block of flats or an archaeological dig, there is the same problem of sacrifice. Here any confrontation with an Arab on one side and a Jew on the other, turns sour. Who would be thought objective in these circumstances? Half-a-dozen old people watched from an upper window, their arms hung out between the bars, they crowded together, gazing at us. Looking at them was like looking back centuries.

A volunteer, a new immigrant, had such stiff hands after his first day's work he couldn't open the marmalade at breakfast. 'I felt such a fool asking my mother to open the jar,' he confided. We walked back together through Jaffa Gate where green hills spread before us in the sun. 'Look at my country. How beautiful it is.' He went on to speak of friends he had left in London. 'I try to tell them what they are missing but they don't care. They are wholly occupied with themselves.' An American girl who volunteered to work for a week, lasted two-and-a-half days. Her social life did not allow her to be on the site by 7 a.m. A young Israeli volunteer whose whole family had been massacred by Arabs (except for his father who had been saved by an Arab friend) answered when I asked, 'How do you feel about the Arabs?'

'I hate them.'

'Do you still see the Arab who befriended your father?'

'My father goes often but I don't like to.'

'How do you feel about Arabs in Israel?'

'I think they should not be here.'

'Will you be compared to a Nazi if you turn them out?'

'No, because the Jews were not trying to destroy Germany. The Arabs wish to destroy Israel.'

Our Masada archaeologist was now digging in the Old City at another site. His small team of Arab workmen greeted me in English and told me the archaeologist was expected back soon. He arrived in high spirits having just learnt his wife was pregnant. They had decided to have four children. 'In this country one might be killed in a war. God forbid! We could not stand it if we lost the only one.' He spoke Arabic with his workers. For one, he translated a letter, making himself as approachable to this team as he had to ours. I found myself telling him about an observant Jew who spoke to me. 'I couldn't believe it, he had such an innocent face with pink cheeks and blue eyes. I had on my only long-sleeved dress, the one that looks so modest. I thought he was lost and wanted to ask the way. It was the way to my house he asked.'

'Impossible! Still . . . that's the thing about Judaism, each man is his *own* judge. He tried for you and failed. One can't criticize. It's for him . . . .'

Our archaeologist had just returned from reserve duty behind the Egyptian lines with a UN team looking for the missing. 'I read maps and tell them where to dig. Our group is a special team, we are all friends. It is a real *mitzva* for the Orthodox to recover the Jewish dead, so they are willing or glad, to help. If it was otherwise, I could not do it.'

His work completed for the day, we walked to the car-park. I had been to the dentist and accepted his invitation to a late lunch. After meeting me at the door, his wife asked, 'How is England?'

I couldn't help commenting, 'Quite far away.'

'For us it is a matter of life or death it is not too far away. The Arabs will kill us if they win a war. Why are we hated for wanting to survive? Do *you* think we Jews are bad people?' I could only shake my head. Gentleness and goodness radiated from her.

Her husband said, 'For peace we would do anything but if we give up one town, one hill, then they fight us one month later. I would prefer to die fighting than slowly, slowly, lose everything before they kill me.'

We rested after lunch and then went to visit mutual friends nearby. Their children rushed out to greet us, once they had made certain who we were. The mother had been teaching them never to pick up anything in case it might be a bomb. After an incident, the biggest problem was explaining to the frightened children that the Arabs, also, were human, she said. They showed some slides taken at Masada; the professor's hat and shooting stick on his bed, water-falls during the great rain, volunteers peering dubiously into 'plaster' sandwiches, a man sitting facing the camera, ('killed in the last war'), and some shots of Ben Gurion's visit. Our exclamations at the sight of a friend in the following pictures made the children shout, 'Ben Gurion!' as if the name were synonymous with the delight we expressed over other slides. It was on leaving that our hostess spoke for us all by saying, 'Those days were like a dream, weren't they? How carefree we were then.'

The walk to work was an enjoyable part of the day with sunrise over Independence Gardens and a stop for fresh bread in the passages of the Old City where early-delivery donkeys met nose to nose and he-hawed with instant love. Few Arab children playing there went barefooted since the invention of cheap plastic sandals. A transistor blared loudly in each open café. 'Allah!' cried the woman

'Allah!' chanted the record's male chorus. The scent of spices, the smells of garbage, a picturesque scene, a scene of squalor, this mixture one found on the way to the wall. Coming out of the tiny passage into the open square where people already prayed at the Western Wall one could hear the fainter sound of a bulldozer around the corner at the Southern Wall. What we would find hadn't become important, being there had.

Interest in the excavation gathered momentum. A fence had to be built to keep visitors out of our trenches. Interviewers came during our precious half-hour's rest. 'Why are you here?' The tape-recorder turned while we answered between mouthfuls of food. 'Don't smile while you work, it doesn't look natural.' The photographers wanted action. After the photographers, it was a general who visited us in an unadorned uniform but with a look of competence, such competence, that look could never be forgotten. I remarked on the lack of ceremony for V.I.P. guests and Professor B. made the gesture meaning that in Israel eveyone's head is the same height.

'An extraordinarily interesting thing happened . . . .' Professor B. would begin and we would listen, hooked. 'A most dramatic place . . . ,' he would tell us and we would believe him though earth and a few stones were all that lay before us. On a rainy day he took us, we weren't too many then, on a tour of the Dome of the Rock. We were like an exuberant school-party. 'It's an anniversary: five years since I've been to a film.' Professor B's mood infected us. 'If you think about it, every day is an anniversary!'

A well-known Zionist spoke to us, stressing the importance of learning Hebrew. It was true, however much I talked to people, not unless I spoke their language could real understanding be reached. Being able to talk French with the refugee workers from Arab countries made a great difference. 'Do you eat pig?' they asked.

I said, 'No, I don't.' Reassured, they sang the *Marseillaise.*

The Swedish theological student obviously deep in thought, hacked at the earth like a hungry chicken. The kibbutznicks' songs made us cheerful. The English volunteer came back with melting ice creams for us during our break. 'This is the first time I've really dripped,' sweat was rolling down his nose. Two Dutch volunteers who had worked in different areas, drifted together.

'It's so long since I spoke Dutch,' the girl explained. 'You know, it's the only language one can really tell jokes in – one's own.' They were all wonderful workers who made the team, held it together, and kept it going.

Finding gold was the event of the day. The workers continually asked, 'Where's the gold?' They could not believe we were taking so much trouble to dig up smashed pots and broken walls. Then Moshe, a gnome-like hunch-back, found a handful of Turkish gold coins. It was the most exciting moment of his life. He sang, he danced up and down, his woollen cap had two pointed corners like ears on top. One worker, jealous of Moshe's luck, whacked him, and three others jumped on them. Knowing they wouldn't hit a woman, I tried to separate the fighters. Even held apart, they spat in the direction of each other's face. Only when they were divided by different deep trenches did peace return to our area.

'Why did you fight?'

'He cursed my mother.' Moshe panted furiously. At breakfast the worker who had started the fight looked at me with loathing for interfering. Leaving, he glowered at me.

I said, 'Shalom.' It was the magic word, and a smile broke over his face.

Each of the refugees was a character who caused either a shudder or sigh of relief in the morning when I saw with whom I would work. 'The Pilot,' so nicknamed because of the goggles he wore, was the worst. Drilling roads in Tel Aviv had made him deaf. No one understood him. He looked too old and too small to be strong though actually his strength and stamina were phenomenal, disastrously so. If a pick-axe did the job quicker, he would use one to hook a pot-sherd out of the trench wall. What he missed with his ears he made up for with his extremely sharp eyes. Floors, he wanted to tear through until we emphasized their importance. The idea that people lived on them long ago made him doubtful, then fascinated. To get him to hear anything I had to yell. 'Stop screaming. We can hear you!' friends would beg after I had been working all day with the Pilot. To slow him down I devised various tricks such as sending him to fill the water-jug or using the big tools myself, or telling him to go to the WC, all of which just made him cackle with laughter. We began to work out a system of communication; each fact or suggestion I got through to him he appreciated and wanted to learn more. One day I knew that with the Pilot by my side we shared two brains and four arms.

The nuns at the hospice still called me, *'Pauvre Chèrie.'* Though no longer cold and wet, I now arrived hot and dusty after work. Dora, a volunteer at the wall, wanted someone with whom to share her flat. I moved in immediately.

Dora lived in the new city and loved the old. We walked to work together. On Fridays we heard the tentative miaows from behind the closed shutters of Arab shops. An Arab guide leading an American Jew to the Western Wall, was telling him, 'You know, you have an *Arabian* face.' Children

154

surrounded the drinking fountains, soldiers prayed, tourists took pictures.

'I don't know why,' Dora began, 'I'm not religious, but since I've come to work here I've been praying at the Wall every day.' We were glad to see the Pilot had arrived in his palm-tree-patterned shirt, his crossed-guns belt-buckle and goggles. His devotion to Ben Gurion, Professor B. and Moshe Dyan was well known, he never tired of trying to tell us about it. Every morning Professor B. came to our area, humming to himself. He would give the Pilot a cigarette and greet us all.

In turn the Pilot toured the excavation and in sign language would report to me that workers were stealing coins, smashing walls, losing floors so as to give the impression of utter desolation outside *our* area. The workers, who had thought of him as a joke now regarded the Pilot with awe as he came from the shed with half-a-dozen pick-axes over one shoulder. Our small team didn't need many tools but the Pilot thought we should have a choice and take the best.

One day many coins and copper objects were discovered, fifty of them in our section and the workers were allowed home early, at 2 p.m. Days or weeks might go by between important finds, then we would come across a great column, or a fine silver coin, or, the nicest of all, a little lamp. This pottery lamp, its face pressed against the Southern Wall, decorated by a minora, seemed to have been placed purposely in position. Traces of Jewish life continuing in Jerusalem after the destruction of the Temple moved us.

On my way to or from work I used to pass the *Eastern Gift*, a shop near New Gate, owned by two Arab brothers. One afternoon I asked them if I might hide a moment in their shop as Moshe, finder of the Turkish gold coins, was following me. 'Who is it? Who is bothering you? Tell me and I will beat him!' The brothers' protection was not necessary, I assured them. I hid inside the doorway and Moshe passed.

Learning I dug at the Wall, the owners of the *Eastern Gift* wanted to know if an antique of theirs was genuine. I admitted I knew nothing though this piece 'felt' wrong. The question had been a test, the next was sincere. Were we really excavating under El Aqusa mosque in order to destroy it as rumour said? Rather than protest, I invited them to come and see. 'We will tell the guard at the gate you owe us money so he will have to let us in.'

'Goodness, say you are my friends, and you will be allowed to enter.'

The brothers, Palestinians, complained that in the war King Hussein of Jordan would not trust them with guns. 'If he will not trust us, how can we love him?' As for the forthcoming Israeli Independence Day parade, they had decided not to go. 'We will do as the king tells us and stay at home. Who can say if there will be trouble? God knows.'

The old Armenian who sold books, newspapers, antiques and souvenirs, like many in Christian Street, had his own problems. 'What I fear most is a Holy War. Not the bombing,' he told me. 'In a Holy War even friends are enemies. Danger is everywhere . . . . The Israelis look at us with superiority, they come through the streets singing. We do not feel as humiliated as the Arabs because we Armenians are Christians, but the Israelis have to learn co-existence.' In his opinion, 'Christianity is losing ground.' He turned to me, 'You are an example. You are becoming pro-Israeli. How can *you* judge them, you haven't lived here!'

'I'm pro-*people*.' I insisted. The Armenian exchanged weekly visits with Israeli friends from whom he had been separated until, after twenty years, the recent war had reunited them, and the whole city. 'They, my Israeli friends, spare me from even saying, *Shalom*. They know that politics are not the fault of either of us.'

'Isn't conversation with them difficult after twenty years?' I guessed it must be.

'No, they are educated, intelligent people.' As you are, I thought. Being part of a minority, whatever one's religion, created problems.

Dora and I found a fairly modern impressed tile in the street, and while we both thought it would be an amusing 'find' to plant on a new volunteer, we agreed that we no longer did things like that. A couple of days later a clearly impressed tile turned up in my area of the dig. Sure that it came from Dora, I hardly looked at it though I automatically put finds on one side to be checked by the archaeologist. The Pilot, noticing it, took the tile to Professor B. who was always near. They returned together. '10th Legion is clearly printed, isn't it? The Romans left many of these but this is a particularly good example. Could you point out exactly where it was found?' I could. I admitted my fault. 'You *will* recognize one next time?' Professor B. wanted to know. I called for three cheers for the Pilot, and the others joined in. He glanced up a moment and gave a quick smile.

Although Professor B. hurt his leg he kept on working until he actually collapsed and was carried away. We went to see him in Hadasa hospital in a room overlooking the central square. No detail of our day's work could be left out, he was interested in everything. His parting words were, 'Keep well!' On the way out we met half-a-dozen others going in to see him.

The reaction at the *Eastern Gift* to the professor's accident was, 'Bring the finds to us, sister. 50-50 profit. Why not?' The elder brother pulled down the lower lid of one eye, the ultimate gesture of conspiracy.

The Moslem quarter of the Old City, the quarter I liked least on Friday, their holy day, was when youths hung about with nothing else to do, 'Fuck. Fuck,' some suggested. I was glad they had not learned whole sentences. The old Armenian and I, making a tour of the city wall one Friday, met a boy with a giant pregnant lizard. The boy killed it in front of me by cutting it and squeezing out its young. He laughed at the speed with which I turned away.

The air-force was practising for the Independence Day parade, its screaming Mirage jets seemed to scrape buildings, then shoot upwards, trailing streamers of coloured smoke. A red-haired American-Israeli parachutist on guard at Dung Gate talked to me, 'I'm too old, I'm twenty-five, the rest are eighteen, twenty. That makes all the difference. It's really tough training but it's something belonging to the best. I'm really proud. For anything special they call on the parachutists, you know. You have to be good. I live in Jerusalem though of course we can't go home. We learn to do without sleep or food.'

'May I buy you an ice cream?'

'No, thanks. You see we exist in a war situation. People think we are loafing here but it is great when the news is quiet and we can take it easy.'

Tanks for the Independence Day came in at night. Friends

took me to watch these grotesque machines driven by boys who looked so young. It was like a bad dream. I had to remind myself that these were the means by which the Israelis could protect themselves. I was too soft, too ready to sympathise. I was a witness, never an equal, in Israel. To get the balance right, I think you needed to be a Jew, needed to have your back against the wall, to take the same view.

The actual parade was gay with millions of blue and white waving flags, marching units of men and women, and planes flying in the Star of David formation. White horses (how dreary to call them 'grey'), with waved manes and tails, followed the President's car. Smiling and suntanned, Moshe Dyan received a standing ovation. I thought of the last parade I had seen, a funeral in Baghdad. The soldiers of the guard of honour wept into big black handkerchiefs, and the high-stepping white horses, frightened and out of control, disappeared backwards between the mobile cannons. Piercing screams of the women were terrible.

This parade over, the old woman originally from Germany, who had sat by me, commented, 'Today we are strong. We can be proud.' I walked away. I happened to pass the place where the terrorists' house had been blown-up. A neat square of bare ground remained, the garden was in flower. On a nearby door someone had painted a swastika. Others, returning from the parade, saw me scraping at it and took over with vigour. One spat on it. We might have been a marauding gang, loose on the empty streets but we weren't. A few Arabs sat on shaded balconies, other Arabs remained out of sight, indoors, while Israeli families picnicked in Independence Gardens or walked along singing. Why couldn't everyone be enjoying himself as he wished? Justice was my obsession. What was justice? 'Only God knows,' was the only point on which everyone here agreed.

I asked the old Armenian bookseller if he had been to the parade. 'No, I barricaded myself in.'

'Against what?' He raised his hands heaven-ward and changing the subject, offered me a plateful of fresh mulberries.

At the *Eastern Gift* the younger brother was excited over a good buy. He was sweating, his hands shook picking up the Roman tear bottles. I asked, 'How much did you pay? They are lovely.'

'Don't talk to me about money!' he retorted. 'How could I resist such a piece! Glass is better than girls ... perhaps there is one girl who is better than all the glass ....'

The elder brother enquired, 'We hear you work not for money, for what?'

I hazarded, 'Inspiration.'

'Where is that?'

'Be men of peace.'

'How can we?' he demanded. 'Last week we go to Gaza to buy fish. The Israeli policeman said he would have to watch my car all the time it was parked because it had Israeli licence plates and might be blown up. *Mine*, an *Arab's* car!'

'Well, who is to blame?'

'Nasser!'

If I talked about objects in their shop to the Armenian he would refer to the *Eastern Gift* brothers as, 'Those melon-sellers.'

'No,' I would say, 'they have an instinct for antiquities, they love them.'

'They know more about vegetables. Ask them! Ask anyone! Going to see your melon-sellers?' would be the old Armenian's parting remark on days I had not been sufficiently appreciative of *his* shop.

It started in the straw-market: a sudden clattering and thudding reverberated on the shops' tin awnings, awnings that almost touched across the narrow streets. As though it were raining cats, they slithered down walls or leaped from windows. An Arab policeman who looked after the city's cats came from the butcher's carrying a plastic bag. He made a peculiar noise through his teeth as he walked. At the first corner and at every niche where they could eat, he dropped handfuls of offal. Following him, the tidal wave of cats grew. What a mewing and spitting there was! A patrol of four Israeli soldiers, *uzis* ready, remained expressionless as cats by the dozen cascaded around them. The policeman called to me, 'A hundred cats! A hundred cats!' I followed. Was he insisting I see the whole lot? He had the permanent benevolent smile and smooth face of a wax-work. At the last stop, outside the police station, a single fat cat sat unmoving, and to this, his own animal, the policeman introduced me with such a punctilious manner that I said, 'How do you do?' His unreal smile shone in my direction.

Professor B. was out of hospital and a guard followed him, carrying a chair in case the professor could be persuaded to sit down. 'This coin is in even better condition than the last!' Speaking with enthusiasm, Professor B, toured the site as if giving and receiving gifts.

The existence of the original Herodian pavement we hoped to find had been verified a hundred years ago when a Captain Warren, an Englishman, completed a difficult survey of Jerusalem. We were going down, next to Warren's exploratory shaft hoping we would find the paving stones farther on.

The Pilot, who kissed the Wall, was capable of smashing stones that had fallen from it with his sledge-hammer. The Herodian blocks came from the Second Temple area wall, gigantic pieces which lay where they had been pushed at the time of the Temple's destruction in 70 CE, we had to explain, because, of course, at this depth the stones almost completely blocked our descent. With increasing awareness he understood. One mud-covered block the Pilot cradled in his arms like a baby to inform me how good the find was. He had made a funny noise to attract my attention. 'Ginge,' was what he called me. Declining a brush, he picked the earth off by hand. 'It's *very* important,' Professor B. exclaimed. 'The stone is from the Temple courtyard. It must be. Every stone is important to us now, more than the pavement you are coming to.' He showed us pictures of the sort of architectural fragments he expected. This block, finely carved with leaves, was of the same quality. 'Find more!' cried the professor. He made you feel you would.

As we dug deeper we had less and less space to move between the fallen blocks. Soldiers gave up their leave to help remove buckets of earth. Everyone questioned us as to when we would reach the pavement. How much farther? The biggest stone blocking our descent had been carved in an unusual shape with a niche on one side. I could not move it, or understand it. The architect sat looking at it for a long time. Architectural problems absorbed him, he would forget to eat or drink. If I handed him my water-bottle, he would finish it. If I suggested he take a rest, he would say, 'But you agree, don't you, it's too interesting to stop?'

The next morning he returned to the site clutching a bar of pink soap. I had never seen him so happy. For a quiet man who didn't raise his voice or talk unnecessarily, his repeated exclamations of 'wonderful' even excited the Pilot. 'I was sitting in my bath last night thinking: as we can't turn the stone over I will cut the soap in the shape as far as we know. When I had, when I could turn it in my hand, suddenly I understood. This stone was on the top south west corner of the Temple mount. Do you see this indentation? This is where the priest would stand blowing a trumpet, to usher in the Sabbath. Isn't the shape beautifully designed?' After the dust had been brushed off, he saw a Hebrew inscription on it, and translated for me. 'To the place of the trumpeting.' Witnessing such moments made me love the country. In Israel the quality of which I was most aware in people was love and, as far as I was concerned, if I couldn't respond, I couldn't really be there.

The others went home at three o'clock. The assistant archaeologist, the Pilot and I stayed. Digging carefully for the last few centimetres, the Pilot reached the pavement. We cleared a small section and saw it was not level. Blocks falling from the top had jolted the paving stones out of place, the archaeologist explained. A journalist hanging about, called from above, 'Any news yet?'

'No. No news yet.' Professor B. must see it first. We covered it again.

Back in the office the Pilot, given a bottle of wine and extra wages, then departed, kissing his hand to us. The archaeologist took off his sandals and ate a *filaffle*. I asked for Warren's 1867-1870 survey book and read, 'The pavement stretches from the base of the pier to the Sanctuary wall, at the level of 2245 feet. There is a pavement of blocks weighing about half a ton each. They are highly polished (probably by traffic), and have a fall, slightly to the East.' I felt great respect for Warren going down that small dangerous shaft to such a depth.

* * *

A section of the pavement was cleared as Professor B.

161

watched. 'Didn't you think it would be there?' he demanded. 'Are you so pessimistic?' he laughed. We must have been looking very serious. Few knew what was happening; when they heard, news spread quickly. The first journalist to join us was a young American. 'What does it *mean?*' He sat down on a stone.

'The Jews have not seen this road leading to the Temple for nearly two thousand years. Perhaps they feel they have come back, come home, when they stand here again?' I pointed to burnt wood, crushed under the fallen wall. I held out some, 'From the year 70.'

'But it's so *fresh,*' the reporter declared, touching the charcoal.

I added, 'There was a coin on the pavement here, dated the year 67.'

A photographer asked me to take his picture. 'How do you feel standing there?' I wanted to know.

'Jewish!' was his response. One archaeologist came to pray. A PR man described his feelings as, 'Great!' and went on, 'You know, this is everything for us. We have no Stratford-on-Avon, no Westminster Abbey.' A journalist who had come to write a story, wept. He had lost his mother and six brothers in concentration camps, of all his family, he alone had escaped. Here he felt he, 'had something left'. However another visitor commented, 'They knew it was here, why all the fuss?'

The President of Israel was going to visit the site. Professor B. asked, 'Will it be clean in time?' It would, just. Armed guards mounted the office roof. Policemen and a flurry of photographers preceded the President's car. Limousines with darkened windows drove right up to the trench. The President, oblivious of the hand-clapping that greeted him, stood above us, on the edge, looking down solemnly. 'The President of Israel wants to say a word to you,' proclaimed Professor B. There was silence while everyone regarded the floor and the stones. Still with our brushes, we stood at one side. '*Shalom,*' said the President.

'*Shalom,*' we said. There was another moment's silence. The Pilot kissed his hand to the two above us, then the cavalcade departed.

'We heard something was found. Gold?' The brothers at the *Eastern Gift* stopped me. 'Was so much talk just over a pavement?' Noticing we looked no smarter for photographers, the younger brother commented, 'You dress in old clothes, you don't care but it's all right, I can't explain why.'

The elder brother nodded at a mini-skirted girl in the street, 'Look at that. If you see it all, it's cheap. I like expensive things!' he slapped his knees, giving me a look. 'Jews from Europe or tourists, live like dogs . . . going with women, clothes half-off. We who live here, or Jews from Arab countries; *we* are civilized.'

The younger brother interrupted using a serious tone of voice for the first time, 'Why do you like Jews?'

I replied, 'They have compassion, courage . . . .'

'That's not a reason! No one has courage. In war we are all afraid. *The same!*' he cried.

Just then a Swiss who identified himself as a pre-history archaeologist, came into the shop wanting to buy antiquities. He chose two of the worst fakes, paid and left. I looked at the brothers' smiles. The younger blurted out, 'But he didn't *ask* if they were real. He *knew* everything. Such insensitive people don't deserve good things. Even *you* knew they were fakes!'

'What a pity he didn't ask. You could have taught him a lot,' I said.

'I *did* teach him a lot,' the younger brother of the *Eastern Gift* remarked.

My Finds

The honour of being invited to work as a volunteer at Hazor and the announced near-completion of the season at the Southern Wall were my reasons for leaving a loved and familiar site for a strange one and staying on past my usual date of return to England. The Professor Yadin who had excavated Masada, had also excavated in Hazor ten years earlier, and had wanted to return; it was July of this year before he could.

One of the hoped-for finds of the new expedition was the ancient city's archives. First mentioned in Egyptian papyrus of the eighteenth century BCE as an important town, Hazor had been beseiged, captured, destroyed and then rebuilt twenty-one times. In the tenth century King Solomon fortified Hazor with casement walls and built a complex city gate. The professor had found an identical gate at Megiddo, another fortified town mentioned with Hazor and Gezer in the Bible as having been built by Solomon. Water was always a primary consideration for any settlement, and a huge city such as Hazor must have had access to a supply in time of siege as Megiddo had with its famous water shaft. As the fortified gates were identical, would Hazor have the same type of water supply, a shaft connected with an outside spring? Such a tunnel or shaft was another of the professor's anticipated discoveries.

Our work concentrated on the upper tell, or artificial hill on which part of Hazor had been built. Not a breeze stirred the dust. Thirty-five degrees was a common temperature. Whereas in Jerusalem we had gone home early in very hot weather, here we worked whatever the weather and finished at lunch-time anyhow. Crawling, persistent sweat dripping between my breasts felt like beetles. A harmless black snake, two metres long, that must have lived there years, had to be killed before the workers would take up their tools. Then the miserable old refugees from Arab countries who had been given the job of digging, looked only for excuses to rest. As the archaeologist observed they went to the WC to hide.

Surface stones were removed, digging started very slowly. Morning after morning the professor, sitting on his shooting stick, watched. Absolutely nothing, not a sign of human existence appeared apart from a rusty bully beef tin or two. We called this hollow on the tell the 'Depressed Area'. I thought we would be better employed on a kibbutz.

Our team lived in Rosh Pina, a village seven kilometres from Hazor. The apartment building was new though the violent wind had a way of breaking all the windows, but just to have rooms of our own were luxuries after having shared tents at Masada. Our house was on a grassy hill with a view of Mount Hermon. We were woken at four a.m. and left fifteen minutes later. Trails of eucalyptus and cypress followed the roads or hid the houses of early settlers. Then the Hula valley dark with crops and trees looked like a river.

'The test of will-power, for me at any rate, is getting up in the mornings. I could easily sleep until eight but after all life wouldn't be interesting without a challenge,' the professor remarked as we walked towards the car. What were his feelings, I wondered, when he came in sight of Hazor, was he proud to have revealed much of its past? 'Not proud, pleased. I often think about the Englishman, Garstang, who first excavated here in 1928. By the time he had ridden his horse over from Sfad every morning, his Arab workmen might have destroyed a couple of levels but he did well with what he had. He was a real character. I went to Liverpool to try to read his original notebooks. They had been bombed during the Second World War.'

We arrived at the tell. The staff were Israelis, naturally Hebrew was spoken. I understood enough only to sense what I was missing. Though I learnt words, I couldn't hear the difference between some letters, let alone pronounce the guttural sounds and my flat, cold accent made even new immigrants cringe. 'Do you have to?' the archaeologists asked when, in an affort to communicate, I padded out my

Hebrew with French or Arabic not understanding how offensive this could be. Later I learned just to keep quiet.

* * *

The professor decided a bulldozer could remove top soil from the 'Depressed Area'. I was transferred to the Solomonic casement wall, an area cooled by breezes. The sun, the warm earth and big coloured umbrellas under which the archaeologists wrote their reports made the change seem more than a transfer: I had been sent on holiday. Twice large flocks of storks hesitated over Hazor, black and white wings unmoving as they swirled in a spiralling cloud until an instinct prompted them to continue their journey. The Solomonic double walls had been strengthened by Ahab filling the casement with stones and the slow process of carrying buckets and sifting earth made little progress, we felt, yet seeing a photograph of the same spot taken a week earlier, surprised us with the change that had taken place.

Instead of going straight back to the house, one morning the professor showed us the early settlement of Rosh Pina. On top of the hill the tiny synagogue with windows the shape of the Star of David was still used though the rest of the neighbourhood remained now half deserted. 'They got tired of the hill and gradually started living at the bottom.' Cypress trees, planted sixty or eighty years ago on either side of the front gates, towered above the single story houses. Even the cobbled road, patterned by alternating blocks of black basalt of the region and white stone looked as though it had been built by people who cared.

Dinner over, the professor divided a watermelon which we ate outside in the cool evening air. He advised, 'I wouldn't sit on the ground if I were you, the scorpions . . . .' A student sat on the ground and was bitten by a black scorpion, luckily not the more poisonous yellow variety.

Fridays we finished work half an hour early at eleven-thirty and rushed to be in and out of the showers and swallow lunch because the cars left when their respective Tel Aviv or Jerusalem passengers were ready. Before the Six Day War, Jenine and Nablus had been Jordan, the year since the towns had become part of Israel's West Bank and a road had been

166

opened so one could take a short cut to Jerusalem and this is the way we went. Arab villages, usually clustered around a minaret, and built on a hill, blended against the landscape. The towns, on the other hand, were not appealing from the main road and my gaze provoked hostile stares as we drove through.

I always went to Jerusalem where a room in a hospice in the Old City was reserved for me. Next door the Holy Sepulchre bells rang with unbelievable bangs and crashes. The muezzin's first call to prayer from the mosque opposite was given, when in diminishing darkness, a black thread could be distinguished from a white one. Though prepared, I never quite took these night noises for granted.

My room had an orange mat on the stone floor, a purple satin quilt on the bed and a photograph of the Portland vase on the whitewashed wall. A Danish boy, working as a gardener, used to bring in a few rose buds for my room. 'Some are dying before they flower.' He was going blind and couldn't see the greenfly on the bushes. His mother was Jewish, his father Catholic, the school he went to, being the nearest to his village, Protestant. 'How were you brought up?' I asked.

'Terribly,' he said. He used to be a painter, now the doctor forbade him to read more than half a page a day. 'I like sailing and ski-ing. I think I will do sport next year. I will not come back here. The Old City is no good any more. It is one big mass of souvenir shops, rubbish shops. Well, we have seen the best of it.'

I wanted to say, 'I'm glad you have.' He was a kindly boy.

Two of the other guests, girls from a kibbutz, were Danish also. 'We came here today and met our first Arab,' they told me. 'He spoke to us in the street and asked if he could show us around. He was helpful and so friendly. We felt we had a real friend, a lot different from what we expected Arabs would be like. Really, he was very nice and went to the trouble to bring us all the way here. Well, at the door I jokingly asked, "How much?" and he said, "Five lira, each. You have the cheap rate." I could hardly believe it! He had been so *friendly*.' What type was he? Was the Arab boy bewailing the fact that a pretty girl had offered him money or was he laughing at her for following him and paying?

Though I tried not to hear them the conversation of two English visitors was amplified by the long hall. 'I had a terrible time getting rid of the Jew I met. I hate Jews.'

The second girl retorted, 'I hate Arabs.'

Thinking it over, the first announced, 'I hate both. *I'm* a Christian.'

The other, 'I am too, not a practising Christian, though.' One of them left to keep an appointment with an Arab who had promised to show her the pool of Siloam. Before she went out, she stopped by my chair. 'Do you think it's safe?' She nodded her head towards the street.

'Absolutely,' I replied. Would travel broaden her mind?

I dined with friends whom I had known since they had lived in London. Their Jerusalem flat was scented with honeysuckle and their garden filled with red pomegranate flowers the first time I went there. It was lovely. They called the garden 'old'. 'All the city will be like this when plants have time to grow.' For a month the husband had been on reserve duty in Gaza. The nights were cold, the days very hot. He told his partner on duty, a peasant, about the stars, but the man's only response was to warn my friends that warts would cover his finger if he pointed at the heavens. 'All his superstitions dated from Biblical times!' The wife, not so lyrical, drew attention to the fact her husband had lost weight, his jeans were falling off and that he was covered with flea bites. His peasant partner had not been affected by fleas at all and my friends added happily. 'It was wonderful. The fleas were the worst enemy there. Thank God!'

Saturday's bread I got from the Kurd's bakery. Puff-ball shaped loaves inside the ovens went flat when brought out on long wooden paddles. Even the Arab shop-keepers from whom I bought nothing said, 'Good morning,' and shook hands. They were accustomed to my interest in the city. It was the 'modern' Arab I couldn't stand, those who yelled at me, 'Hi, Hippy! Smoke hash? Sell blood? I give twenty-five pounds.' Their equivalent lurks in every big city.

The youghurt was late in my usual grocers and so distressed was the Arab owner by my being kept waiting, he invited me to share his breakfast. How long had he been in Jerusalem? 'One hundred and fifty years,' came the prompt answer. I said I wished he would be there as long again and a smile replaced his worried look.

An Israeli stopped me in the street. I didn't know who he was until he finished speaking. He said, 'I've been thinking. You are right. The pavement at the Southern Wall *is* something to get excited about.' Then he went on his way, leaving me open-mouthed in surprise. He had been one of those indifferent excavation visitors, one of those who had challenged us, 'Why all the fuss?'

'What have you brought us?' asked the *Eastern Gift* shop brothers. I was ashamed to have been away and then come back carrying only bread. They enquired about the health of my father, for, since the brothers had given me seeds for his garden, I was the bearer of messages between them and him. To create the impression he was in a good mood, the elder brother praised Kissinger's peace efforts but this was to soften the ground for what followed. 'The poor Armenian, he is an old man,' the elder brother began, his eyes half closed. 'He buys cheap African figures, leaves them in the Dead Sea and sells them later covered with incrustation as Roman.' The extent of his fantasy revealed the extent of their undercover rivalry.

'How did you know I know him?' I asked.

'We are not blind.' Considering their shops were streets apart, this was an understatement.

Though only guards would be there on Saturday I wanted to see how the Southern Wall excavation had progressed. Despite their intention to stop, the dig had continued and grown. Many people in David Street were going the same way to pray and in the crowded passage an Arab carrying a bread tray on his head accidentally knocked an Israeli woman. Screaming, she toppled the loaves onto the ground. The crowd stopped, anger or fear showed in their faces. A poor Bedouin selling bottles of multi-coloured sand was wedged in the middle. Fortunately another Israeli pulled the woman away and ended a potentially nasty situation.

I couldn't resist buying a ripe melon and took refuge in the peace of the mosque courtyard to enjoy it. A child watched me cut the fruit. I held out a piece without looking at him. It was accepted silently. The child crouched by me, eating. The silence, the cool stone, deep shadows and royal blue sky were fantastic. I remembered the snow and how cold and wet my feet had been during my first visit.

After a warm greeting, the guards at the wall invited me to share their picnic lunch already neatly laid out on a blue plastic table cloth. They described the recently discovered mosaic floor with pride. Pointing to a row of faces at the fence, one said, 'We have to keep out tourists or they get in and break their legs. Of course they are convinced we are guarding some secret treasure.' That was true and to the guards everything was treasure.

Three Israelis, also touring the excavation, afterwards offered to take me to an antiquities shop. When we arrived, the Arab owner, a friend of theirs, got out his special stock. A silver shekel, year one, Herodian lamps, spearheads, weights, a fibula; the owner produced one article after another. Next he brought out a gold hoard that no one had seen. Smearing his hands symbolically over his face, he committed us to absolute secrecy. Earrings and a matching pendant set with blue stones in pure gold were just a part of it. Then he showed us a model in solid gold of a man and woman making love yet so static and stiff we had to look again to be sure that's what they were doing. The hospitable Arab, delighted at his success in entertaining us, brought forth another parcel done up in tissue paper. Unwrapped, we saw it contained chocolates for us. Our faces must have dropped at the anti-climax.

* * *

On Saturday evening the Hazor car picked me up at a café just outside the city walls. Roads were deserted at sunset in the former Jordanian territory through which we drove. There were no lights, few vehicles or Arabs to be seen after dark. Our car spluttered, on one hill it stalled. The night was depressing. Taking out a revolver and loading it, the archaeologist commented, 'If you want peace, be prepared for war. It's a Roman proverb.' He smiled at me.

At last we crossed the old frontier again, Israelis strolled along Tiberius' brightly lit and busy streets. The air was balmy and there was a full moon. We dined at a café so close to the lake's edge that carp ate the crumbs I threw them from

170

our table. It is at odd moments like these that one counts one's self ridiculously lucky to be alive.

* * *

Near Hazor the professor strode towards squatting women, kittens, chickens and children who filled the path, confident that a way would open for him, and it did. We followed the professor across a nearby field to inspect the ancient water channels. An eager young student turned to encourage me, 'Come along. It's adorable!' Not an adjective I would have used to describe a possible sewerage system though I wished I could make myself understood in Hebrew as well as he did in English. It was a privilege to be there and not getting and not giving as much as possible was a terrible waste. Frustrated by my ignorance, aware that my understanding was limited, it was only much later, after reading the professor's book on Hazor, that for me the site took shape.

Bedrock with cup marks, cut out hollows for holding pots, had been reached in the Depressed Area. Might we be nearer to finding a water shaft? The professor was sure we were. Quite a few people had each bet him a case of whisky that he would find nothing. From the professor's past record I would have supposed they were feeling generous. The professor hired a giant crane to clear the debris cut out of the hollow. 'It works like three hundred workers,' his eyes twinkled. 'No, like four hundred,' the professor corrected himself.

Finds that turned up daily in our area with the pottery were usually simple ones. The Israelite inhabitants of Hazor three thousand years ago had not been rich. We did find a small bronze snake and I remembered, 'Moses made a bronze serpent and set it on a pole and if a serpent bit any man he would look at the bronze serpent and live.'

Now I worked in the palace where ancient mud-bricks could seem like part of the soil. Learning to detect them was the most subtle digging I ever had to do and for that reason I enjoyed it immensely. On one side, fourth century Persian graves intruded, skeletons and burial objects had to be painstakingly removed before we could progress. Our new worker thought it a waste of time. He talked to Avraham, the

171

wheelbarrow man, in French and nodded towards me at work, 'What do they find? Nothing. Me, I'm from Egypt. *Chez-nous,* we have all the treasures. Since I arrived this morning she's been working *comme un folle.* What for? They don't pay us enough. Why should we work?' Avraham cautiously agreed.

Thick plaster on a wall suggesting a room of importance interested the professor. 'Good, we will open that section and find the corner.' A platform, pieces of incense-burner, votive offerings and a few animal bones appeared. An old worker was showing me a game he had played as a child with similar knuckle bones when the archaeologist came along. What he wanted was a clay tablet, the archives! 'A bottle of whisky if you find even one!'

'But I don't drink.'

'Then you'll begin!' exclaimed the archaeologist. What was incense in French? I wanted to tell the new worker from Egypt about the incense-burner. The archaeologist explained how far he thought the floor of the room would extend and he wanted it covered carefully with sacks before we left.

'What is "sack" in Hebrew?' I asked.

'Sacks is Hebrew. It is a Biblical word,' he said.

This archaeologist, while questioning me about England, asked about 'my people'. I had never considered I belonged to a group. No bond exists, no joy is felt by simply meeting another English person. I referred to us as flotsam and jetsam, the term puzzled him as much as its meaning. Prompted by the news of fresh explosions in Tel Aviv and Jerusalem he said he would be in Israel thatever the conditions. 'We have been hated thousands of years. It is human nature. It won't change. What will change is us. They have been accustomed to the defenceless, cringing Jew. Now we are going to be strong and fight, at least for our lives.'

'How can you stand the continual worry?' I asked.

'I will tell you a story,' he answered. 'A landlord threatened his Jewish tenant saying that he would throw a man and his family out into the street if the Jew didn't teach his dog to talk within a year. The Jew went on quite happily. People asked, "Aren't you going to try to teach the dog? Aren't you worried?" He replied, "No. Maybe when the time comes the dog will be dead. Maybe I'll be dead, maybe the landlord will

172

be dead." I'm like that. I don't worry until problems are like this.' He held his hands in front of his face so he couldn't be seen.

Periodically archaeologists went to do their annual military service and others helped out in their place. I had the job once of showing around a journalist who complained, 'Israel is such an awfully militaristic country.'

'Self-preservation,' I replied. He was writing in his notebook and didn't respond.

A couple of Syrian Migs landed voluntarily twenty kilometres away. We had not heard the reason though soon everyone learned the good news. Patrolling Israeli jets swooped over the tell with a scream of speed and dipped their wings as a way of saying *'Shalom.'*

* * *

The weekly trip to Jerusalem was never boring, though for the staff, tired, hungry and longing to see their families, the journey was always too long. The strange craggy hill we passed were the Horns of Hittin where Richard suffered final defeat on his crusade. In the hot sun I could imagine the crusaders roasting in their armour. We gave a lift to two soldiers, the dark one sang, glad he would get home for Friday evening, the blond one said he spoke six languages. A hot wind whipped up waves on the lake called Kinerette and Galilee. Banana and cotton fields bordered the shore. The white cotton balls were being harvested and taken away by tractors drawing big wire cages full of them. We drove through Jenine again. The scarecrows in Arabs' fields were dressed as Arabs which was natural, for a moment it caught my attention. We passed a burnt-out tank left from the last war. Here ancient tombs had been exposed by road widening. Once we had a vision of the far-off sea and all along the route Arab boys sold figs, freshly picked. The highlight of the drive was choosing some and gorging ourselves on the green or black fruit.

* * *

I had washed and was going to visit Dora when the 'Jesus

173

man' in the hospice introduced himself. Upon hearing my name, he didn't say, 'How do you do?' but, 'Praise the Lord!' So I asked if God talked to him every day. 'Of course,' he assured me, 'you know I've tried drugs, Buddhism, sports and photography, but it's only Jesus who Saves.' This wide-eyed innocent-looking American youth confessed, 'In Vietnam I killed men.'

An archaeologist had once warned me, 'Beware, there are more weird types in Jerusalem than in any other city. I was on the Temple mount and a man I had never seen in my life came towards me his hand outstretched, crying, "Elijah said we would meet!" '

I rushed over to Dora. 'I'm sorry about the news.'

'Yes, the kittens died, they weren't well anyhow.'

I exclaimed, 'The explosions!'

'Oh that. That was *last* week.' I was glad to see her. Another girl shared her flat since I had left for Hazor. they would both study archaeology when term started. We exchanged news of our respective digs as Dora was still at the Southern Wall. I had brought them flowers from the Old City. Dora's friend pointed out that they were not really fresh, 'You can't trust Arab flower-sellers in the Old City,' she reproached me. I had picked them out myself, I was to blame for not being more careful, I told her, thinking of Steve's efforts to make better relations between Arab and Jew. If only he had not returned to England, he and Dora would have got on well together.

I described the tension caused by the petty incident between the Israeli woman and Arab baker in David Street. Manners are important to Arabs; I was sure he hadn't pushed her. 'How can we be hypocrites?' demanded Dora, 'Manners are very good but one must not have them for their own sake. If we are always honest, the Arabs will know us as we are, they will trust us to say what we mean.'

The other girl had come from Czechoslovakia to England with her family and from there to Israel. 'I'm not going to move again,' she declared simply, 'I don't want to live anywhere else in the world.'

Dora agreed, 'In the last war I thought we would win, if we had lost, without Jerusalem, it wouldn't be worth living.'

At the Christian Arab's shop another of my films had been developed. He and his friends were drinking arrak while a

174

blind musician played a mandolin and sang to them in Turkish. He went on to sing in Greek and Armenian. When I asked for *Jerusalem the Golden* he gave a perfect rendering of *My Country 'Tis of Thee*. The owner held a glass of arrak to the musician's lips. Behind the mirror glass door was a dirty WC and a rolled up Jordanian flag. It was not a shop in which I talked more than a few minutes or ever sat down, nor was I invited to.

By seven, night had fallen with a suddenness unknown in England. I walked through the courtyard of the Holy Sepulchre on my way to buy youghurt. Donkeys waited outside the church, monks in the shadows lit lamps that made the old stones gleam. At the sound of music I entered and listened to the service. An Israeli policeman, who thought my being there alone unwise, followed me at a discreet distance. A priest in a red cassock and big cross paced the aisle with an incense-burner, at each shake, red coals glowed, scent, and a puff of smoke came out. He shook the burner twice in front of me. Was this good or bad? A little man followed carrying a candle almost as tall as himself. After the service they kissed one picture, then another, and then crawled under the altar to kiss one more, performing the ritual with compulsion, their expressions fervent. The brass roses, the dim red lights, the painted faces of the watching saints enriched their worship. I had to remember, with so many individual forms of expression, that we share a basic conviction.

The loud nervous laugh of an American visitor demanded attention. That evening I was reading in the salon of the hospice when she began to talk, unencouraged. As if she had to, she informed me she had come through Amman in Jordan, 'I felt sorry for the refugees, I even wrote things against Israel before I had been here. I realize it was a silly thing to do.' She was confessing to a complete stranger, the first person to whom she had really talked since her arrival in Israel a week ago, and I would be the last here because, as she said, 'I'm catching my plane back to the States, Sunday. My ticket is from Tel Aviv, that's why I'm here. I was so nervous when I came to Israel, I thought they would throw me in prison. I was shaking, honest.'

'That won't happen. Why did you write what you did?' I asked.

'You know, I wanted to hear my voice on the radio. It's great to read what you've written in the newspapers. It meant meeting a lot of interesting people. I saw a lot of refugees. It makes me sick when Israelis talk about *their* Promised Land.'

'In the Bible it is promised. Anyhow, the Jewish workers with me on the dig have lost everything after being made to leave Arab countries. The Israeli government gives them jobs. Instead of letting refugees fester in camps wouldn't it be better for Arab governments to give them jobs and homes too?'

'Yeah,' she began uncertainly, 'I shouldn't have written what I did but you get so involved here. At home in the States you have so much leisure. You're not needed; what you say doesn't matter. There everything is settled, here it's all happening!' She laughed loudly, 'Why are you here, to escape the Establishment or for archaeology?'

'Neither exactly,' I said. 'I like it.'

Walking down Christian Street the next morning to get the newspaper from the old Armenian, I ran the gauntlet of salesmen with nothing I wanted. An Englishman I knew was having tea with the Armenian and the shop was already crammed with Italians choosing postcards. Each one of the group, to show they were together, wore a giant wooden cross. Since my experience of sleeping in Petra and digging in Jerusalem I was sorry for these quick tourers who might never get a second look. An Armenian, a crony of my friend, who helped out in the shop, poked through the cards and found the one he wanted for me. 'Look, this was taken when the good Christians were here.' He showed me the photograph of General Allenby in front of Jaffa Gate. 'See if you see your family.' I looked earnestly at the accompanying British officers.

'No, I don't think so . . . .' The shop's postcards might be of the same age monument with, on the back, 'Printed in Palestine', 'Printed in Jordan', or 'Printed in Israel'. During Ottoman rule their postcards were sometimes 'Printed in Egypt', and when I was there these fascinating cards remained in the boxes among newer ones which the public preferred and bought first.

Baked eggs that had an excellent nutty flavour were served

with my tea. 'Eggshells were found in an oven at Masada. Is this how they cooked them?'

'Yes,' the old Armenian said. Archaeology was the way to his heart, I had discovered.

The Italians left and then an absolute rogue of a Bedouin entered with some pots in an orange crate. 'Rubbish,' the Armenian declared before he had even looked at them. The Bedouin was told to get out. After many exchanges the Bedouin sat fanning himself with the hem of his robe, the pots on the table before us. His eyes rolled as he swore on his mother that the pottery had come from under the ground near Hebron and that they were not fakes. He also had seven or eight bracelets in a dirty handkerchief. Choosing two pots, those with the clearest grooves, the old Armenian took the bracelets as well. Winking after the Bedouin had gone, he told us, 'It was worth buying the pottery to obtain the Roman bracelets. The pots aren't bad though . . . Byzantine,' he tapped one thoughtfully. 'I don't know how the Bedouins do it. They go straight to a place, mostly at night so they are less likely to be caught, and dig where the tombs are. No one can explain it. They might have buried the objects themselves by the way they know the place. It's genius. If we tried, we would dig in several spots and only if very lucky, hit something. The Bedouins have instinct, that's it.' His crony pranced around rattling a jug. 'Maybe there's gold inside.' The shop-keeper retorted, 'That jug is Calcolthic. They didn't make coins then.' The man, not a bit put out, grimaced and nudged me as if to say, he has no sense of fun, has he? I told them how hard we worked to find a little piece of Roman bracelet. The Englishman who had remained aloof from the proceedings until then, said he could not understand my being a volunteer or working for low wages. He had a 'good' job and thought I should have one too. A friend of his needed help and would pay me well. I was curious.

'What would I do?'

'Supervise.'

'Do they use donkeys?'

'No, Arabs carry the buckets.'

'Would I dig?'

'No, they have trained Arabs to dig who come every year.'

'Oh. Would I supervise the workers?'

'Not exactly, there's a foreman for the workers. You would supervise a section of the dig.'

'Oh.'

'I believe the last person who had the job carried a little brush and brushed things, and er, a notebook, of course.'

'I'm not qualified to write reports.'

'The Arabs are really quite decent to work with.'

'I know they are but I'm used to the democracy of the Israeli excavations.'

'Odd you say that. I find the Arabs have a larger concept of humanity. I see Arabs resentful and humiliated as Jews march through the Old City to pray at the Wailing Wall. It's like an invasion. I can't help thinking, poor Arabs.'

'Don't you think everyone should have the right to pray at his own holy place?'

'Yes, but I can't help thinking poor Arabs, they look so forlorn.'

'If praying at the Wall meant everything to you and you were not allowed to, would you think you were treated humanely?'

'No, but I . . . .'

After Shabat I would say, 'I'm so glad to be back,' and at Hazor, the archaeologist would be amused.

'Did you have a good time?'

'Yes,' was all I could say. How could I tell them more, how could I explain 'my people'?

* * *

The professor's friend and driver looked at his watch and rushed out of the straw-roofed shelter where we were having our 9.30 breakfast. He had to light the smoke-signals for the helicopter's landing and already we heard the roar of its approach. It circled with a great glass eye cocked down at us. He lit the flares. Thick dust disturbed by the blades engulfed those who ran towards the machine. For a few seconds nothing was visible. Guests the professor had brought with him came into the shelter and we poured tea for them. One opened the professor's packet of sandwiches. 'I'm afraid those are the professor's,' I warned her.

178

'Oh yes, I just wanted to see what he eats,' she said. Another roar denoted the helicopter's departure taking the professor up again to photograph the site. One of the archaeologists hit a suspended spade head with a metal bar, our signal to return to work.

Avraham, from his seat in the wheelbarrow, urged the others to wake. As a Jew he had been forced to leave Casablanca six years earlier with his mother and three sisters. Avraham talked lovingly about the Moroccan beach. 'Here I work, I eat, I sleep. *Il n'y a pas de distractions,*' he complained. Once the helicopter came low and again raised piles of dust. Avraham and I waved, the professor waved back, and then it landed.

'Did you like flying in it?' I had not been in a helicopter.

'I didn't have time. I had to take photographs so fast. I wanted one from every possible angle. Normally, yes, I enjoy it very much.' The professor had flown to Tel Aviv and returned at 2 a.m. Even with only two hours sleep he was in excellent spirits. No wonder the woman wanted to see what he ate; what gave him such energy.

The team was anxious to co-operate when they were awake though they had an enviable ability to relax into a dream state. Avraham came to me, *'Le Vieux,'* he pointed to a man with a long white beard, 'he went to synagogue last night. Take work easy.' 'Captain', our sifter, leaped to attention if I asked him anything. He liked finding pottery and showed me every piece yet given a moment he could go to sleep on a loudly playing transistor. He had ulcers. The problem was his stomach, he explained, 'Now I have not the force. The life, I watch. In Israel it is hard.'

The men passed full buckets up the ladder to the sifters and Avraham wheeled away the unwanted earth. I would fill twenty or thirty buckets and when they finished sifting them, the men would rest while I prepared a new lot. At the end of the day Avraham pointedly remarked, 'We like working with you, even though we have to work hard.'

Two young, fat, ugly, vipers in our square were the first thing I saw one morning when I moved the wheelbarrow. The professor was soon on the scene, 'A real viper?' he teased, 'What we want now are the parents.'

179

'Do we?' My knees were still shaking even after the archaeologist had killed the snakes. 'Small vipers like those aren't dangerous, they merely cause discomfort. Only the large ones,' the archaeologist held his hands as wide apart as they would go, 'kill.' Walking across the tel to breakfast he put the transistor to my ear, 'The latest Beatles' record,' he said to take my mind off the snake population.

The professor's driver and friend used to combine funny and sad remarks or say serious things as though they didn't matter. 'I wish Moses had led his people to Switzerland. What did he do in those forty years? Brought them here where there have always been wars and always will be wars. My father had to fight. I fight. My sons will have to fight. The back of my car is full of guns and ammunition. I'd rather have it full of watermelons.' In the mornings I noticed innumerable varieties of bird or animal footprints in the soft dust, creatures of which we were not aware, that had come out after we left. Every trace of them soon vanished under another onslaught of our work, those small prints like the driver's thoughts, once formed were lost; existing briefly then blown away.

* * *

On Friday evening when I came into the hospice, the watch dog, growling and barking frantically, hid behind me, the hair on her back bristled like a cat's. 'Why, she knows me better than anyone,' the Jesus man followed her, holding out his hand.

Changing direction, he set his sights on me, 'Why don't you pray for a husband for yourself?'

'Don't you think it is wiser to pray for others' happiness? One gets one's own rewards, anyhow.'

'Amen.' He had given up trying to convert me since he realized I believed in God as firmly as he did.

'Why does the dog bark at you?' I asked.

He was serious, 'She knows I'm trying to get the Devil out of her!' Another guest entered carrying a loaf of bread from which, all day, he dispensed little bits to everyone he met. The Jesus man eyed the crumbs falling over the carpet as the boy tore off a piece for me.

'No. Thank you. No, thank you!' The Jesus man, his bland face upturned as if longing for divine patience, waved the boy away before he could approach.

The *Eastern Gift* shop was empty except for the younger brother who raised his hand in a welcoming gesture. Suddenly a man with a walkie-talkie entered and behind him came Moshe Dyan. The bodyguard offered me a cigarette, another kept looking up and down the street while the general examined antiquities. The price of the Iron Age pot and javelin heads wasn't right, he wouldn't buy. He looked at me with a smile of utter charm. No one else was allowed in the shop until the guests had vanished as quickly as they had come. The brother sighed, 'All are my friends. Even your father likes me.' He went and stood by the door. 'See here, the open sky. My shop is a prison sometimes. Last year I went to Egypt.'

'How did you like Thebes? Weren't you impressed?'

'Yes, but most of the time I was sick. Sunstroke. Beirut is so cosmopolitan. I'd like to have my business there. Here it is so boring. You can't imagine how boring it is, Sylvie.' I told him there were times I felt the same in London, though we had Hyde Park in the middle of the city with a lake, boats and horses. He wanted to know how much horses cost an hour. I told him. 'It is a fair price. An hour is enough, you become tired . . . . You know I like to do business with Moshe but he shouldn't be such a hard man.' Was his sad expression to win my sympathy? He looked at me, 'Excuse me if I ask you something. I ask you like a sister. Aren't you terribly lonely?'

'No one has asked me that. Yes, I am.'

'When I was in Egypt I was terribly lonely. I have known love. She is the most beautiful woman I have ever seen. She is Israeli. She was far more experienced than I. I was madly in love with her. I think, for a while, she was madly in love with me. I have loved many women but this one, this one had everything.'

'What happened?'

'I found her morals, her policies were not mine.'

'Are you a practising Moslem?'

'Some think I am not religious. I knew this case was hopeless. I've thought of suicide . . . .'

181

'I understand.'

'Let us say it is the government who are sick, not us. Those peaches are very sweet.' With nostrils quivering and with trembling fingers he picked another out of my basket. I was examining a dish full of Bedouin rings and found one with a red stone that fitted my finger. He noticed. 'Take it,' he said. 'Take it! I give it to you.'

Just as I was slipping back through the hospice's big doors I heard a call and saw the American girl volunteer who had worked at the Southern Wall Excavation two and a half days. 'Hey! I was coming to your place to see you. I've had a traumatic experience: I've sold my car.' Like many ex-volunteers, I ran into her from time to time. 'Israel used to mean something to me when I first came here. Now I'm in the depth of depression; there's a sort of veil over my eyes.' Obviously she needed to talk. Depression? I had forgotten what it was months ago.

'Let's go to a café,' I turned back in the direction of David Street. She continued as we walked.

'I've made up my mind to return to the States. I don't want to see anything to keep me here.' A small boy nodded to me in passing.

'He is the tea boy at the *Eastern Gift* shop.' I mentioned the fact to distract her.

'Yes, I know. I had a passion for the younger brother.' The awe in her tone of voice amazed me. 'I used to find excuses to go in his shop all the time. He is always very polite. I asked him out for coffee once but he looked at his watch and said he had a "meeting". I even took my mother in. We stayed about an hour but no dice.'

'Aren't you Jewish?'

'Oh yes. I've taken every sort home though. My mother says, "Darling, I want you to be happy".' The girl described several Arab boyfriends she had had, 'Even during the war.' She asked, 'Do you remember the Independence Day parade? We were on the wrong side of the road, my boyfriend and I. We had to cross between tanks to get home. It was horrible. The whole business of the parade .... He took me to his house once. I think his parents knew it wouldn't last. Arabs are so closed, you can't really get through to them. He got so he only wanted to come at night. he felt uneasy about going out with me. Arabs are stubborn, boy, are they *stubborn!'*

'Did you experience persecution as a child?'

'Not much. Usually I was richer than other kids in the neighbourhood. Two years I spent in a convent. It was something for them having a Jew there. I said rosaries for them.' By then it was a dark, windy evening. She thought she had better go. I accompanied her to the gate of the Old City. As she left, she left me with a question, 'Being Jew and Arab together was sort of ideal. Wasn't it?'

* * *

'Sweets from Jerusalem!' The Hazor workers shouted in Hebrew, making me feel as I took out the bag that I had bought them something special. They just hadn't tasted Opal fruits before and adored them.

The refugee worker who had come from Egypt tired me with his chatter. He was moved to the top of the ladder. There he was silent and miserable, our company cheered him, so down he came. He talked about his business in Egypt, how he had employed many men and how, after living in Cairo for forty-five years, he had his passport stamped, *'Aller sans Retour'*, for being a Jew. He felt too old to start again and accepted labouring jobs to get out of the house. He was an educated man who became both fond of, and good at, our job.

To suppress desolate memories and to occupy the time during work that meant nothing to him, the small, round, French-speaking refugee he-hawed like a donkey so well that this noise coming out of a deep trench transfixed visitors. His black eyes would stare, he began by breathing heavily the way donkeys do, he might stamp and paw the earth, one almost visualized a tail whisking. The sounds were too realistic: when I hear a donkey now, I think of Shimon. His he-haw would finally trail off on a melancholy note to the applause of other workers.

When 'Captain', our sifter, arrived, he turned a wheelbarrow on end, took string out of his pocket, hunted for a piece of cardboard and tied it on the wheelbarrow's handles thus making a sunshade. He then sat under it to wait. In

September he arrived in a big black hat, 'for the winter.' As the weather got no colder, he finally returned to his khaki cap. He had a lined, joyless face but he greeted me every morning, the words cheerful, the expression a death mask. He looked over the edge of the trench at us as if into a grave.

The weather, though hot, was better than it had ever been in mid-summer. One could see to the horizon, the air was intoxicating. For cooler evenings the cook wore a sweater over his habitual bathing suit. He was thin with round black eyes and a long moustache drooping at the ends. A man of many skills, some liked his cooking, everyone admired his carpentry, and like most of us, he had been at Masada. The worker known as *Le Vieux*, he reported, slept in Synagogue. Why did we work him so hard? I said, *Le Vieux* slept all day, I had thought it was so he would be rested enough for Synagogue.

The cook did not care for cats or cooking but fed us all well. Usually cats haunted the dustbins; Lulu haunted us. Even before the professor put down his broad-brimmed hat on a bench beside him she would be there, she frequently found herself under it. She was black and white and very fluffy with the ugly splodged markings of a cheap Japanese toy. She was an idiot and voiceless, able only to mouth miaows. With a vacant expression she ran to whomever called her. People kicked her or gave her peppers to eat but she never learned from experience. Lulu was not popular with Wimpy either. Wimpy was the second black and white cat. Mostly pink with mange, Wimpy, grotesquely stiff, sat in wait under the table and when Lulu bounded past, lashed out. The burst of spitting and flying fur made everyone jump. At the start of the dig, Lulu came to us matted and dirty, she became immaculate. The dig finished and Lulu had to return to life in the wild for which she was never equipped.

'Do you always eat so much . . . er, in England?' the professor asked as we had breakfast. If I ate for two, I would have the energy for two, I hoped. The professor had woken everyone, broken into the locked kitchen and made coffee because the cook had been delayed at home. Given more time, I would have drunk enough for three of that excellent brew, I thought but I didn't say so.

Wide descending stairs were uncovered in the great Hazor water shaft. Photographers and journalists arrived, Hazor's water source would be front page news. An American began by asking, 'In your archaeological digging Professor, what have you learned about human nature?'

'That it's unchanged,' the professor replied. 'Same problems of fighting and survival etc. you mean? The journalist's pencil was poised. The professor glanced at him, 'Fighting *to* survive. Survival.'

* * *

At Jenine we saw the same black horse standing under a tree with the same red sore on its back as it had been the week before except that this time was different: we wouldn't be driving to Jerusalem again. The dig at Hazor was over and we were leaving with mixed sentiments. Although I loved returning to Jerusalem I equally regretted an excavation's ending after becoming involved with the land. Now it was left for someone else to discover the archives; to learn about the trials and tribulations of the people of ancient Hazor. Arab students ambled around the countryside, book in hand, memorizing whole passages for their exams. One child waved. At Nablus, Arabs looked at us and looked away. The fig season was over though a few boys tried to sell them. Trees were white with summer dust and everyone waited for the first rain.

The archaeologist next to me in the car mentioned the intermittent shooting near his home in the Jordan valley. I congratulated him on his new son. His wife had moved out of hospital into the kibbutz air raid shelter, he said. He asked me about Turkey. A friend of his had gone there for a holiday. He had wanted to go too. 'It was when I was wounded by the Syrians, I was up to here in plaster,' he pointed to his neck. he talked interestingly of other countries yet seemed immersed in sadness that day. It is as if people sometimes make a moat around themselves after a certain limit of sadness is reached and nothing can be said, for a while, to bridge that gap. Figuratively speaking, one can only raise one's hand and wave in sympathy as if from far away.

We stopped at an Arab café for fruit juice and found

185

antiques on sale. A pottery lamp had a double spout, one Herodian, one Byzantine, a fake *par excellence*. I remarked, 'Isn't that unusual?'

'Yes!' the archaeologist agreed. He mentioned to the café owner that he was an archaeologist and the owner grunted as if initiative was all that job required.

They dropped me for the last time at New Gate and I saw the date season had begun. Such variety was unknown to me: red ones smooth as wood, black shrivelled dates, brown shiny ones. I bought some which disappeared quickly. 'A present for me?' The elder *Eastern Gift* brother asked. Devouring them, he congratulated me on my selection and ability to get them at a fair price. 'Look what archaeology has done to your body. It's ruined it. You used to be all soft and now you are hard.' The elder brother, after his observation, went on, 'You didn't *know*? You didn't *hear* about the Armenian? Last week he died. He very old, very sick man.' He spoke especially gravely.

The last time I saw the Armenian he had been on the way home, we had passed each other at Damascus Gate and after talking a minute, he had remarked, 'You eat so many ice creams one day your tongue will freeze.' Even if he tried not to smile, I noticed dimples appearing in his cheeks.

'Then take it!' I cried. He did, without a word, without looking back, rather bent now, eating his ice cream, he walked out of the city.

'My sister,' the elder brother repeated. I recovered and realized he was still talking. 'My sister, perhaps you are Oriental?'

'Oriental?'

'Oriental girls do not go out with someone unless they are serious.' To my silence he confided, 'My brother is crazy. He want Jew woman, not Arab woman. He has bad luck. Perhaps you are like him. Antiques, antiques, antiques, sometimes I think he sleeps with antiques.'

To every beggar he gave money. One ragged man was ashamed to enter the shop, I transferred the coin to him as he waited at the door. 'It's a secret. Don't tell my brother. I make not a penny today. Because there is trouble, no tourists come.' A horse galloped down the passage.

'What a beautiful Arab horse,' I admired the animal as it

passed.

'It is an English horse. English horse is best,' he said. I got up to go. He needed to be reassured. 'What do people say if they know you have Arab friends?'

'If people are my friends, they *are* my friends. Your brother is well?'

'My brother is in Beirut. Antiques! Would you come to our house?'

'Yes, I would. Thank you.'

Their father, with a Hogarthian greedy face, blue eyes, and very small hands, was propped up on cushions as if awaiting me. 'How do you like Palestine?' was his first question.

'I love Jerusalem,' I replied, trying to keep the conversation from running full tilt into ruin. He believed England and America helped Israel win the Six Day War. 'And England more,' he added with significant looks as if I might divulge the details. 'Johnson was behind the Kennedy killing,' and 'The Jews want to destroy the Old City so they can stand at Jaffa Gate and see the Wailing Wall.' Sentences like the ingredients for a stew, he tossed in, the stronger the better, while his son kept quiet; I had been taken there and tossed in too.

Another idea came to the father, 'Nasser really loves America . . . .' He put his finger-tips together signifying friendship. The mother sat cross-legged and silent. She was old with hardly a line on her face. Her severe and simple dress added to her beauty. A plastic vase of plastic flowers was on the table between us and through them her eyes watched mine. A picture depicting the family tree of Mohamet, a poster of Petra and a large photograph of King Hussein hung on the white walls.

'Israelis also pray for peace,' I blurted out rather too loudly.

'If people say one thing, the can mean another,' the old man warned me. 'What did you think of the Arabs *before* you met them?' I could not tell him I had not thought about them at all. Now I thought very often about their problems.

How awful I felt. Did talking about the crazy world make one ill? What was the matter with me? I tried to make my mind go back over what I had eaten. 'It was an honour to meet you,' I told them. It was. I was grateful for being allowed to look and learn, to go in and out of different worlds though I was opposed to the prejudice there. I was glad to talk, usually, now I felt so sick I could hardly walk. Not knowing how, I got to the hospice and bed, this last time in the hospice's basement.

* * *

'Well, how are you Mr Sylvie, happy?' the servant said in Arabic, meticulously picking seeds out of the half grapefruit by my bed. He flicked the seeds in the direction of the wastepaper basket. Four days had gone by. Being extremely ill I could only nod. My stale sweat smelt sickening. The light of the basement was cold and grey, I imagined I was in England. My dreams were confused, my sleep never deep. The Danish gardener brought me some boiled potatoes and cabbage. I couldn't put the hot food in my mouth. 'You look funny. I call the doctor.' He had gone. Only by crawling did I reach the bathroom. In the mirror I saw I had turned completely yellow.

The stretcher was lowered, 'Lie down.' A blanket was put over me. The men carried me through the narrow passages of the Old City, to New Gate where the ambulance was waiting. On the way I smiled weakly at the elder *Eastern Gift* shop brother who stepped back from his shop door, horrified. Pedestrians, pushed aside by my stretcher bearers, suppressed screams when they saw what appeared to be a corpse carried through their midst.

The little hospital room had a window overlooking a street in central Jerusalem. Nurses wrapped me in a pink towel dressing-gown patterned with the Star of David. The bed was supremely comfortable, I sank on to it; I had never lain down with such relief in my life. 'Zippora,' the blonde blue-eyed girl in the other bed introduced herself. Speaking slowly in Hebrew and a little English, she said she had two children and that they lived in Meashearim. The doctor interrupted.

'A good case of jaundice,' he muttered kneading my naked stomach with cold hands. 'If it hurts so much, why do you laugh instead of cry?' he demanded. I felt ravenously hungry. 'The first sign of recovery,' he pronounced. 'Don't worry if

188

you are depressed. I've had jaundice. One gets terribly depressed for no reason. It's one of the symptoms of the illness,' the doctor warned. Instead I was absurdly happy. The room was the best in the hospital, my neighbour the nicest. The food tasted marvellous. Was jaundice affecting me in the reverse way? I wanted no more than to lie still and absorb the kindness and comfort in this sunny room.

Zippora exclaimed, 'The Beatles!' and turned up her transistor, laughing. It was like being back in the world! How considerate she was: quiet when I slept, good company when I was awake. Of all my friends none would have been such an easy, good companion at this time. She was not ill enough to stay in hospital for long. Every evening her husband visited her. He had side curls and wore the traditional black hat and black coat. Because I was contagious her two beautiful children could not enter, they talked to us from the doorway. I had not seen a closer or more devoted family. Zippora was amazed to hear what other wives in hospital said about their husbands. If her husband returned late at night she was glad, knowing he had been studying. She was modest, not prudish. To miss going home for Shabat saddened her. On Friday evenings she lit candles which illuminated our little room. A rabbi in a golden coat came in to make sure we had put away the transistor.

Did the doctor's comment, 'You're doing well,' refer to my health or the number of my visitors? Dora brought me a reading light and a transistor.

'The Pilot still makes those funny noises and shouts at the other workers. They just laugh now,' she said. An archaeologist who visited wanted to have Arab and Jewish workers on his next dig.

Another described the advantages of using donkeys, 'They carry eight bucketsful *uphill.'*

On the way to the bath I tried to read the plaques in Hebrew on beds paid for by donations. Even the food-lift commemorated a Brooklyn rabbi. Our room was dedicated by children to their parents lost in the Second World War. The nurse who brought round tea had got out of Russia a year before. I asked her how she managed to leave and come to Israel. She said it was difficult, shaking her hand as if she had burnt it by touching something hot.

Saturday evening, when the Sabbath was over, Zippora took out her knitting. She made two sweaters while in hospital, one each for her husband and a friend. She herself did not possess one. Now she startled her husband by greeting him in English. In the afternoon she read a book about concentration camps filled with such ghastly photographs that when she held it out to me I could only cry. Magazines or light reading she considered pointless. She always listened to the news and did not care for de Gaulle or Jacqueline Kennedy.

Only once, for ten days, Zippora had left Jerusalem and gone to Tel Aviv with her children. They went to the beach. She had never seen the sea before and loved it, but it was Jerusalem which was the centre of everything for her. Why should she go anywhere else, she asked, why go dancing or to the cinema when walking with her family gave her such happiness? So her husband could study the Torah she had a job teaching young children. From her I learned more Hebrew than during my whole holiday. Her shy husband finally smiled and said, 'Shalom' to me. He used to fetch us corn on the cob from a street-corner stall outside. Her mother, like Zippora, a warm and generous woman, came back to visit me long after her daughter had left hospital.

* * *

I felt like lingering at Lod airport. Once there, one was caught in the system, the schedule of departure. We took off and seemed to float over vast rushing forests of cloud. The unnaturalness of flying made me very tired. The Alps rose to meet us, their snow dazzling in the afternoon sun. A far away plane hurried in the other direction. It took us a few minutes to cross the Channel. England was full of smoking chimneys, we circled and lost altitude fast.

A girl detached herself from the waiting crowd at the barrier. She was the new one in our London flat, I remembered, and she had driven out to meet me. She helped put my bag in the car and then we were speeding towards London. I noticed the greenness of the grass along the motorway. 'I'm pro-Jewish at the moment, my dear. My doctor's a Jew. He's dreamy,' she gushed. I was worn out.

Perhaps it was the pain of missing Jerusalem? She kept on talking as she drove, 'Mummy and I had such a row in the taxi this morning, we had to ask the driver to stop and let us out, then we had to find another taxi when we'd finished. My dear, we arrived at Harrods absolutely exhausted.' I felt so ill, I could hardly make any sense out of the conversation. 'Susie,' she was saying, 'do you remember Susie? She's just got over an unhappy love-affair with a married man. *Italian*, my dear.'

A wave of nausea overcame me. She glanced in my direction, 'Oh, you poor thing. You'll soon be home and when you feel better, tell us all about it. Your trip must have been absolutely thrilling!' She said it for me. Despite my illness I suddenly felt very strong.

Laughing I agreed, 'It *was* thrilling.'